P9-CRT-687

Low-Water-Use Plants

for California & the Southwest

by Carol Shuler

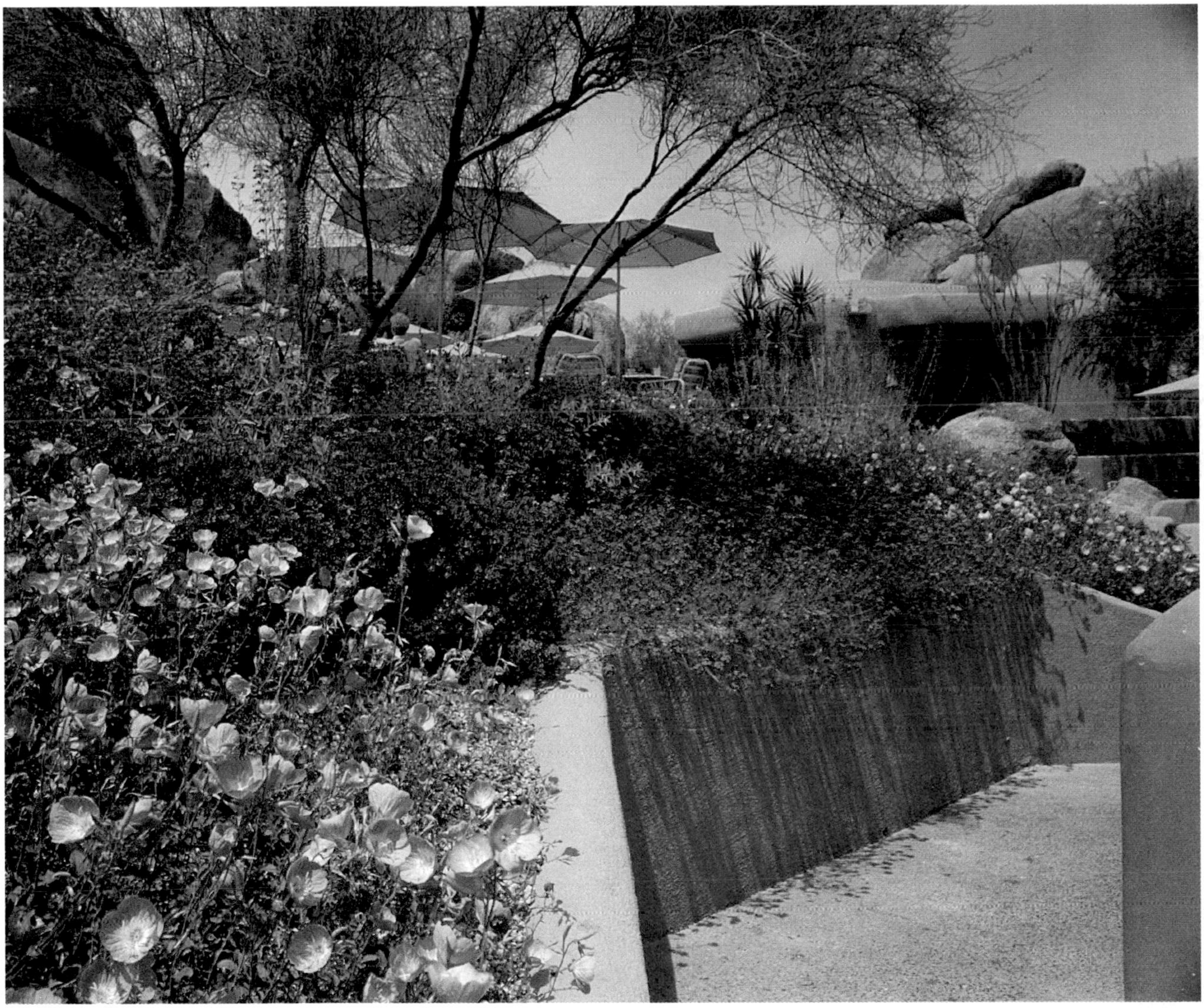

Rich color and texture complement the boulders and overall setting. Boulders Resort, Scottsdale, Arizona. David Hutchinson, designer.

FISHER BOOKS

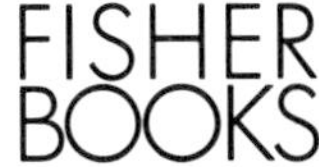

Colorful, low-maintenance ground cover and a spectacular view create a great place to rest and contemplate. Design by Mary Rose Duffield, Tucson, Arizona.

Publishers: Bill Fisher, Helen Fisher, Howard Fisher, J. McCrary

Editors: Bill Fisher, Sheryl Clapp

Art director / illustrations: David Fischer

Design and production: Sheryl Clapp, Paula Peterson, Sean Stewart

Published by Fisher Books
PO Box 38040
Tucson, Arizona 85740-8040
(602) 292-9080

© 1993 Fisher Books

Printed in U.S.A.
Printing 10 9 8 7 6 5 4 3 2

All rights reserved. No part of this book may be reproduced or transmitted in any form or by any means, electronic or mechanical, including photocopy, recording or any information storage-and-retrieval system, without written permission from the publisher. A reviewer may quote brief passages in a review.

Library of Congress Cataloging-in-Publication Data

Shuler, Carol, 1946-

Low-water-use plants for California and the Southwest / by Carol Shuler.

p. cm.

ISBN 1-55561-037-4 : $14.95

1. Drought-tolerant plants—California
2. Drought-tolerant plants, New.
I. Title.

SB439.8.S58 1993

635.9'52—dc20 92-34627

CIP

Fisher Books titles are available at special quantity discounts for educational or corporate use. Special books—or book excerpts—can also be created to fit specific needs. For details please write or telephone.

Notice—The information in this book is true and complete to the best of our knowledge. It is offered with no guarantees on the part of the author or Fisher Books. The author and publisher disclaim all liability in connection with use of this book.

Contents

Acknowledgments
iv

About the Author
v

Introduction
vi

Aloe ferox

Environmental Benefits
of Xeriscape Gardening
1

Low-Water-Use Plants
(alphabetically by botanical name)
5—99

How to Use Plant Tables
100

Trees Selection Table
101

Shrubs Selection Table
105

Groundcovers Selection Table
111

Accents and Vines Selection Table
115

Horticulture
121

Index
137

Acknowledgments

I am fortunate to have so many knowledgeable friends to call on for technical review and advice. Their support and interest in this book are greatly appreciated:

Kent Newland of the City of Phoenix Water Conservation Office, who assisted me with technical advice and review of the manuscript and shared generously his extensive botanical and horticultural expertise.

Ron Gass, owner of Mountain States Wholesale Nursery, Phoenix, Arizona, who provided cold-hardiness information on plants listed in the book and a general review of the manuscript.

Matt Johnson, botanical specialist with the Desert Legume Program, Tucson, Arizona (a University of Arizona and Boyce Thompson Southwestern Arboretum cooperative program) who clarified the confusion surrounding the *Prosopis* species and the latest changes in the genus *Cassia*.

Dr. Jimmy Tipton, arid ornamental specialist with the University of Arizona College of Agriculture, who offered the results of his recent plant-growth research and the impact of this information on horticultural practices and optimum growing conditions.

Greg Starr, owner of Starr Nursery, Tucson, Arizona; Dr. Mark Dimmitt, Curator of Plants, Arizona-Sonora Desert Museum, Tucson, Arizona; Warren Jones, Professor of Landscape Architecture, Emeritus, University of Arizona; Harry Thompson, Professor of Botany, Emeritus, University of California, Los Angeles; and Lauren Bonar Swezey, senior writer for *Sunset* magazine for their review and comments.

I also want to thank my staff at C.F. Shuler, Inc. for their continued support and patience from first draft through numerous revisions for consistency and preparation of graphics.

Carol Shuler

Photo credits

Photos by Carol Shuler except those by—
Judeen Adam: pp. 12, 49 (upper left);
Ron Gass: p. 92 (left);
Warren Jones: pp. 7 (upper right and bottom), 8 (left), 9 (bottom), 11 (top right);
Charles Mann: pp. iv, 5;
Judy Mielke: pp. 59 (bottom), p.60 (left);
N. Scott Mitchell: pp. title, ii, 1;
Kent Newland: pp. 8 (right), 18, 27 (bottom), 30, 33 (bottom), 39, 45, 57, 58, 59 (top), 60 (left), 63, 66 (left), 84, 90, 99 (bottom left);
Chad Slattery: pp. 111, 114 (top left and right);
Greg Starr: pp. 17, 34 (top left);
Russ Widstrand: pp. 83, 114 (bottom left), 121, 122, 134, 136.

Yellow colors in this setting are offset by greys and greens. Cacti provides bold accent. Yellow blossoming tree is a palo verde. Marcus Bollinger design.

About the Author

Carol F. Shuler, L. A. is president of C. F. Shuler, Inc., a landscape architecture firm in Scottsdale, Arizona. She studied architecture, landscape architecture and horticulture at the University of Arizona. Since 1970, she has provided consulting services in Arizona, Nevada and California. During her career, she has resolved diverse design challenges from urban pedestrian malls to riparian habitat mitigation.

Shuler applies the principles of horticulture and ecology in every design for the purpose of achieving climate mitigation, erosion control and improved wildlife habitat. The result, through lowered water and energy use, is a landscape that is friendly to the environment.

Shuler's appreciation of the fragility of the native southwestern environment propels her work. Most of her large-scale projects include salvaging native plants prior to construction for re-use in the landscape. Since 1989, her firm has tagged over 15,000 plants for salvage.

Shuler is a leader in innovative landscape approaches that mesh the expertise of engineers, hydrologists and landscape architects to find environmentally-responsible solutions to site conditions. Her award-winning work combines ecology, horticulture and the mitigation of natural elements such as climate and flood control, earning her a reputation as a pioneer in her field.

Attractive garden of low-water-use plants with whimsical figure. Leshin residence, Scottsdale, Arizona. Designer: C.F. Shuler, Inc.

Introduction

*H*istorically, choosing attractive and hardy plants that thrive in unique arid conditions has been difficult due to the limited availability of both appropriate plants and literature on how to grow them.

Although plant availability has improved in the last few years, most gardeners and landscape professionals remain unfamiliar with recently introduced plants and retail nurseries are hesitant to carry plants other than those commonly requested by customers. The goal of this book is to address this need for information.

Those of us in the Southwest face hostile growing conditions: extreme temperature ranges, minimal rainfall and alkaline soil. Making the right landscape choices allows landscapes to mature and blossom. Wrong choices cost money in maintenance, repair and replacement. Working *with* the natural ecology, rather than against it, creates a natural aesthetic which promotes regional pride and a commitment to preserve and strengthen its energy.

The more than 200 plants selected for inclusion in this book were chosen by a team of landscape professionals including horticulturists, landscape architects, botanists, landscape contractors and nurserymen.

Physiologically, these plant materials share common characteristics. They are tolerant of cold, adapted to our soil conditions and drought-hardy. These shared virtues mean the difference between thriving and simply surviving in arid environs.

All of these qualities would amount to little if the plants themselves lacked visual appeal. The plants discussed in this book were selected to offer a wide range of visual options from strong sculptural qualities to delicate leaf and flower structures.

The intent is to reduce water consumption without compromising aesthetics. This can be accomplished by using plants in their ideal environment so they do not need to be coaxed or persuaded to live.

Water is our lifeblood. It fosters our lives, industries and recreation. To sustain these, we must remain conscious of conserving our resources without compromising our quality of life.

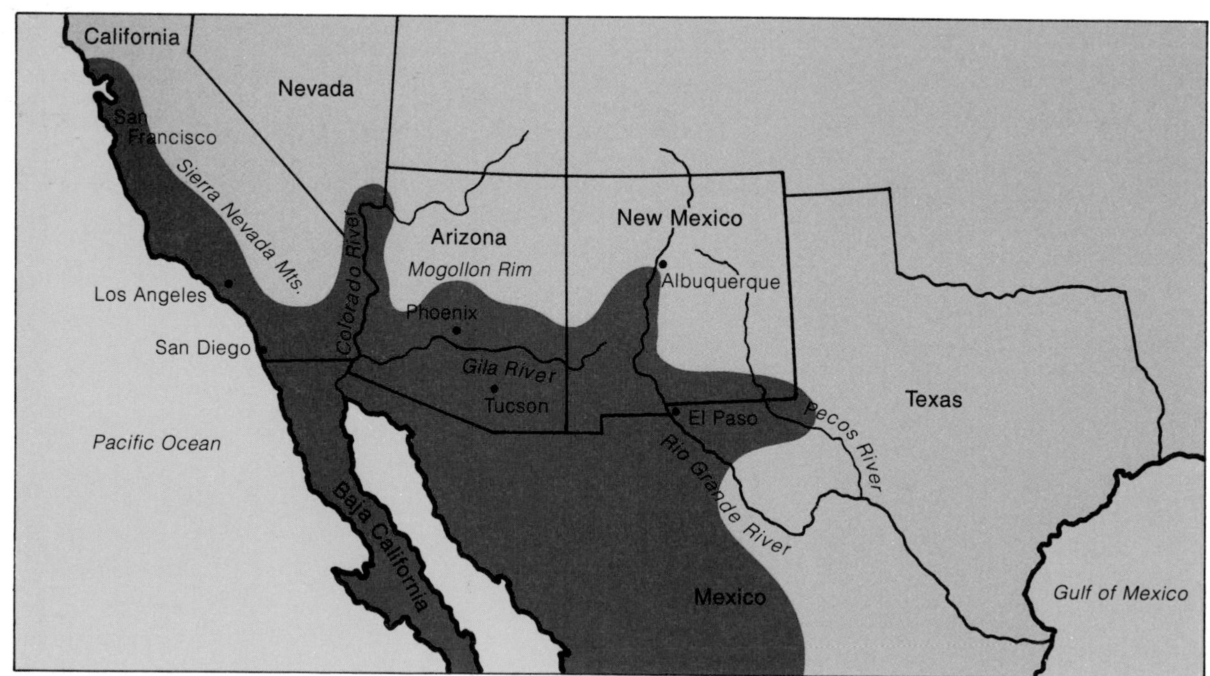

In addition to California and the southwest, the information in this book can be used for arid regions in Africa, the Arabian Peninsula, Australia, Hawaii, the Mediterranean and South America.

Benefits of Xeriscape Gardening

A variety of low-water-use plants selected to give a riparian look around the water feature.

Trichocereus huascha hybrid

Environmental Benefits of Xeriscape Gardening

Most of the southwestern United States has an arid or semiarid climate. In simple terms, this means that large portions of the area are considered deserts: They receive little rainfall and have an evaporation rate greater than the annual rainfall. Phoenix, Arizona, for example, receives between 6 and 7 inches of rainfall annually and has an evaporation rate of over 6 feet. This means that, in one year, 6 feet of water will evaporate from a lake or swimming pool.

Although low levels of rainfall do not necessarily mean drought conditions, periods of drought and dryness are a recurring phenomenon in warm, arid and semiarid climates. In addition, global warming (through the greenhouse effect) may cause more frequent and intense droughts.

With its mild winter, temperate and sunny climate, the Southwest continues to attract both individuals and corporations for relocation. The immediate impact of expanding population on water resources results in serious consequences during dry spells. People, wildlife and vegetation are equally affected.

The reality, especially in the Southwest, is that recurring droughts are with us to stay. To minimize the hardships they cause, we must change some bad habits: excessive water use inside and out, inefficient irrigation, and the overuse of thirsty non-native plants, for example.

We must use our resources more wisely. The results can improve the urban environment and lifestyle through climate mitigation, reduced maintenance costs, improved aesthetics and increased wildlife in urban areas.

What Does Xeriscape™ Mean?

Xeriscape is a term coined (from "xeros," the Greek word for dry) to describe the concept of an environmentally-sensitive landscape. It is a trademark of The National Xeriscape Council, a non-profit organization.

Although the concept is applicable worldwide, "Xeriscape" is interpreted differently according to need in Miami, Florida; Phoenix, Arizona; or Los Angeles, California.

Although lowered water use is the primary reason to adopt Xeriscape principles, many additional benefits are achieved.

Alleviate the Heat

One of the benefits is the alleviation of urban heat. Urban development with its buildings, roads and parking lots causes an increase in air temperature. The rising hot air creates a dome of heat (an urban heat island) over developed areas.

This dome can affect local rainfall patterns by forcing storms around the high pressure (the domed) area. (See Figure 1.) Lowered rainfall and higher temperatures have a major effect on plants.

To combat this island of urban heat, we need to provide shade for as many surfaces as possible. Planting trees is the most effective means of providing shade. Shrubs and groundcovers are also effective in shading the earth to reduce glare and reflected heat.

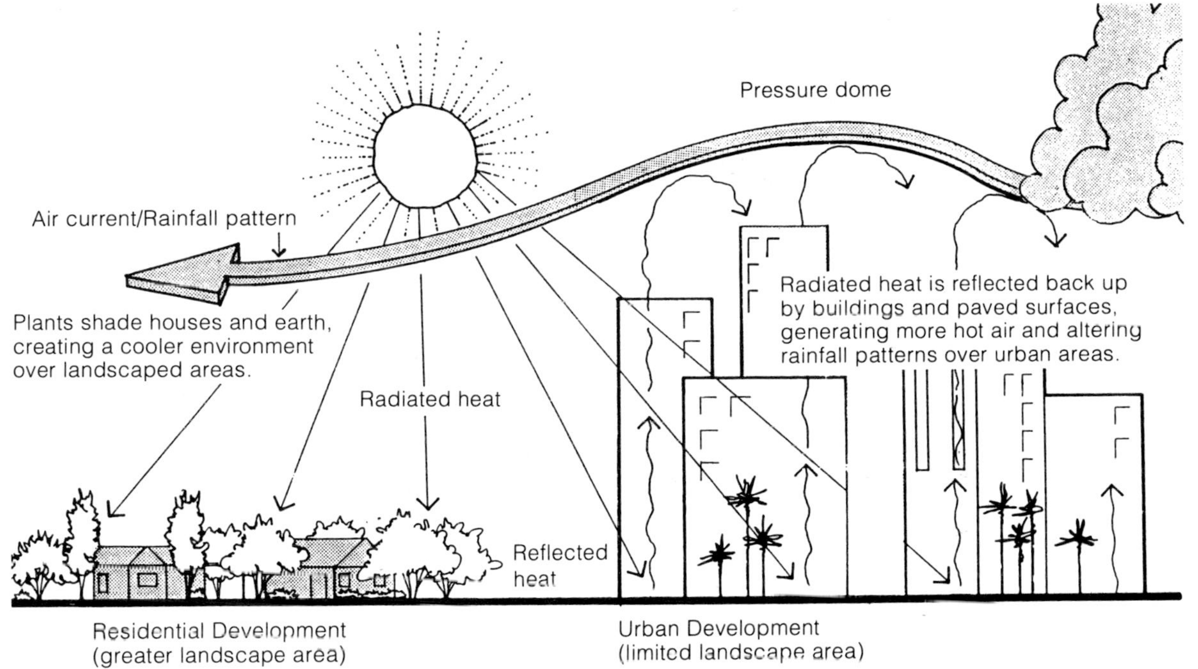

FIGURE 1: ***Urban Heat Island.***

Attract Wildlife

Development also destroys wildlife habitat. Landscaping, particularly with native trees and shrubs, helps to replace habitats for wildlife. Many beneficial animals such as birds, rodents, lizards, bats, butterflies, etc., can adapt to urban life if provided food and cover. These animals can become your own private pest-control army; they are the natural predators of those pesky insects.

If you want to attract certain species of hummingbirds or butterflies, be sure to include the plant types they particularly enjoy. This information is provided in the plant descriptions in this book.

By selecting a wide variety of plant material you will attract a wide variety of wildlife. Vary potential habitats from tall trees to groundcover. Dense, thorny bushes will protect birds from even the most-aggressive house cat. Select primarily native plants as they are the most attractive to wildlife.

Learn which non-native plants are used by local wildlife. For example: Hummingbirds love aloe from South Africa and flowering Eucalyptus from Australia. To attract butterflies you must provide nectar plants for the adults and food plants for the larvae. Yes, they will damage the foliage, but it's worth it. Outdoor living areas are more rewarding when you hear birds chirping and bees buzzing.

Nearly all animals in the Southwest are drawn to water. Provide a reliable water supply for them. Figure 2 shows how to make a simple wildlife waterer.

Locate the waterer far enough from drives and patios so animals will not be frightened. Shrubs for cover should be placed nearby. Leave the area around the waterer fairly open so housepets will have to keep their distance. Expect visits from bees during warm, dry weather.

Harvest Rainwater and Reduce Erosion

Regardless of where in the arid Southwest you may live, it is important to keep as much rainfall as possible on the land. Grade and terrace your property where possible to retain the

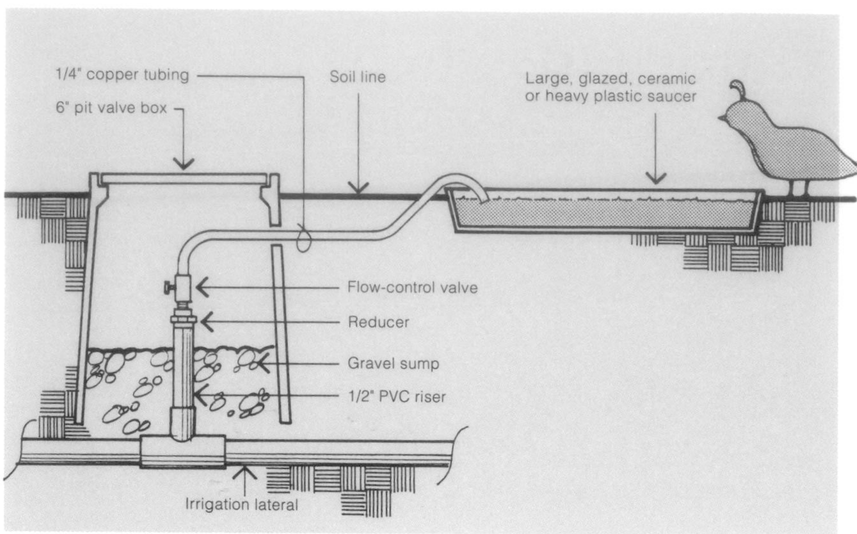

FIGURE 2: ***Wildlife Waterer.*** Nearly all animals in the Southwest are drawn to water. Provide a reliable water supply for them.

water. Slope patios and walks toward planting areas. Walks and patios made from bricks or other pavers allow water to seep through to the earth. Trees, shrubs and groundcover all help to reduce erosion.

If you have a large suburban property, chances are that a portion of it is undeveloped. Seize the opportunity to increase its water retention. First determine sheet flow, the direction in which rain and excess water flows. Then, using an ancient Native American technique, rake some of the surface rock and soil into windrows perpendicular to the flow of the water

If no loose surface material is available, dig little trenches across the flow. Pile the dirt along the downhill side of the trench. This process creates a "speed bump" to slow the departure of water from the land and gives the water greater opportunity to seep into the soil. Steeper slopes require speed bumps placed closer together.

At first this treatment will appear unsightly. In a short time native plants will start to grow in the new areas where more water is available. (Apply an appropriate seed mix to enhance regrowth.)

The first to come will be grasses and herbaceous plants. They will grow into a living system which retains and filters more and more water. Later, trees and woody shrubs will further enhance the water-retention capacity of the area.

Reduce Waste

The reduction of *green waste* is another benefit gained by the employment of Xeriscape principles. Most prunings, clippings, etc. end up in the landfill. Only a small portion of this material is useful in commercial mulch production. Regulation may be required to curb this environmental problem. Reduced-lawn size and careful selection and placement of shrubs help to lessen the volume of green waste. The need for power tools—which use fossil fuels and add noise pollution—is also reduced.

Conclusion

Approximately 60 percent of the water treated for urban use is delivered to residences. Of this water, nearly 50 percent is used in landscapes. With careful planning and an understanding of plants, even those of us living in deserts can enhance our surroundings while preserving our natural and financial resources.

Low-Water-Use Plants

Santa Fe garden with mullein (plant with coarse foliage in foreground), yarrow, Penstemon and native juniper. Plants provide textural interest against colored-wall background in this courtyard. Design and installation by Eden Landscapes, Santa Fe.

Acacia berlanderi with author's dog Boojum

Acacia is a diverse genus from which we may select trees, shrubs or groundcovers. The majority of the species available for landscaping are from Australia. Others are from the Sonoran Desert (Arizona and Mexico), the Chihuahuan Desert, South America and Africa. A. *salicina*, A. *smallii* and A. *stenophylla* are deservedly among the most available and widely used species. The others are harder to find but worth the search.

Acacia abyssinica, Abyssinian Acacia, is a lacy deciduous tree similar to Jacaranda in texture. Growing to about 25' in both height and width, it provides an open canopy. In spring, white puffball flowers decorate this slow-growing specimen, a native to eastern and southern Africa. Hardy to 18-20F.

Acacia aneura, Mulga, is an excellent patio tree maturing at 20' high and 12' wide. The short, slim, silvery-gray, leaves are reminiscent of *Cassia phyllodenia*.

Several times during the year, electric-yellow, rod-shaped flowers appear. Mulga is an Australian native, evergreen, clean and trouble-free. It is hardy to 10F.

Acacia berlandieri, Guajillo or Berlandier Acacia, is a slow-growing, deciduous tree maturing at approximately 12-15' in height. This hardy native of the trans-Pecos region of Texas will grow in any well-drained soil but prefers a spot in the full sun. The minimum recommended spacing is 12-15'.

Acacia aneura

Acacia abyssinica

Guajillo's lush, lacy foliage creates a sub-tropical atmosphere while blending into desert riparian (wash) species. The effect is similar to Lysiloma although the plant is more drought- and cold-tolerant.

Guajillo needs to be grown as a multi-trunk specimen to show off the graceful, gray-barked, vertical branches. When pruned, the cuts yield a gum similar to Gum Arabic.

Lightly fragrant, creamy white puffball flowers are abundant in the spring. A few recurved thorns occur on the branches. Hardy to 15-20F.

Acacia rigens, Needle Acacia, matures as a large shrub at 6-8' in height. The gray, needle-like, evergreen foliage is carried on stiff angular branches. In spring, yellow rod-shaped flowers nearly conceal the branches and create a sculptural effect. Needle Acacia is native to Australia. Hardy to 20F.

Acacia aneura

Acacia salicina (both photos)

All Acacia are good for attracting bees.

Acacia salicina, Cooba or Weeping Wattle, is a tall, slim evergreen tree maturing at 25' in height.

This Australian native has long, narrow leaves, 3/8" x 3", on weeping branches which move sensually with the slightest breeze. Its willowy upright form is a contrast to the squatty, stiff-branched Acacias native to the southwestern U.S.

Deep, well-drained soil is essential for good root establishment. Young trees should be watered regularly until established and minimallly afterward. Staking and guying are necessary during the first three growing seasons while roots develop stability.

Weeping Wattle can be planted as close as 8' on center in groves for an unusual effect. Particularly in the evening, gentle wafts of fragrance come from the creamy, puffball flowers in fall. The drooping branches need to be kept trimmed above any shrubs planted beneath. Low shrubs or groundcovers provide the best understory.

***Acacia smallii (A. minuta)*,** Desert Sweet Acacia, is evergreen and hardy to 12F. Its mature height is 15-20'. Minimum spacing should be the same. It will perform well in sunny locations in any well-drained soil.

Acacia smallii

Although nearly identical to A. *farnesiana*, A. *smallii* is much more cold-tolerant. Fragrant, golden puffballs adorn this tree through the winter when little else is blooming. Its bright-green, fine-textured foliage is similar to White-thorn Acacia, a native of the Sonoran Desert.

Desert Sweet Acacia is native along the U.S.-Mexico border from southwestern Texas to south-central Arizona and is good for blending with native desert trees.

The thorny branches need to be pruned above walkways. Due to nearly year-round droppage, place A. *smallii* away from pools and patio eating areas.

Plant Desert Sweet Acacia upwind from patios, windows or doorways to take advantage of the pleasant fragrance.

Acacia farnesiana

Although sparse, the blue-green foliage of Shoestring Acacia is cooling. Cinnamon-colored bark provides a pleasant contrast.

Acacia stenophylla

Acacia stenophylla, Shoestring Acacia, has drooping, evergreen leaves (actually modified petioles or leaf stalks) which are long and narrow (1/8" x 16"). Its leaves are similar in texture to the Mexican or Green Palo Verde, however the Shoestring Acacia is *not* messy. This makes it one of the best trees to plant near pools.

Shoestring Acacia's tall, slim form matures at approximately 30'. Space them 20-30' on center. This tough Australian performs well in any soil with drainage.

The light shade of this tree is perfect for succulents, flowers and roses which suffer in full sun. When backed by a high wall, A. *stenophylla* creates wonderful shadow patterns. The creamy puffball flowers produced in fall are not showy. Hardy to 18F.

Acacia willardiana (three photos)

Native Americans dried and powdered Acacia leaves to use on diaper rash and horses' saddle sores.

Acacia willardiana, Palo Blanco, is a most graceful and interesting tree. Of special interest is the white, papery, peeling bark.

It needs to be planted in a protected location against a high wall to protect against frost damage and to show off its wispy, weeping foliage and branches. Mature size is approximately 20' high x 10' wide.

The flowers, which are not showy, are cream-colored catkins (scaly spikes without petals).

Native to central Sonora, Mexico, Palo Blanco is hardy to 25F.

Agave bovicornuta

A*gave* are frequently available at specialty plant sales. Some are suitable for pots only. Others may be used in pots or in the landscape. Although it may take years for them to bloom, most Agave die after blooming. Prior to blooming, some species produce offsets around the base. Others, such as the Octopus Agave, form bulbils or plantlets on the bloom stalk. These may be rooted in small pots and planted out when well rooted.

Agave bovicornuta, Cowshorn Agave or Lechuiguilla Verde, is a handsome dark-green Agave which prefers a shady location. Its broad leaves may reach 4' in height. Mature plant size is 4' x 4'. Good drainage is essential. This species, a native of the Sierra Madre of western Chihuahua, Mexico, may be hard to find. Hardy to 19F.

Agave colorata, Mescal Ceniza has heavily "toothed," frosty blue-green leaves which bear distinctive bud printing (the impression of adjacent leaves).

Suitable for large pots or as an accent plant in the landscape, Ceniza should be placed where leaf patterns are easily visible. It offers good contrast with greener groundcovers and background shrubs. Flowers are bright yellow.

Mescal Ceniza is native to central Sonora, Mexico. Its mature size is approximately 3' x 3'. Full sun and good drainage are required. Hardy to 15F.

Agave parryi, Parry's Agave, is particularly attractive and hardy. Dark-brown teeth edge the blue-green leaves which grow in symmetrical rosettes and mature at 2' x 2'.

Once plants become established, offsets will form. These can be carefully removed and potted until well rooted. It performs well in full sun or light shade. Flowers are deep yellow-ochre.

Native to southeastern Arizona, New Mexico and central Mexico. Hardy to 0-5F.

Agave vilmoriniana, Octopus Agave, matures at 4' x 4'. Groups of Octopus Agave cling like spiders to nearly vertical rock cliffs in the Sierra Madre of western Chihuahua, Mexico. Its graceful, smooth-edged, soft green leaves are reminiscent of octopus legs.

Agave parryi

Agave vilmoriniana

Native Americans used the fibers from Agave leaves to make cordage and fabric. The hearts were roasted in pits, then dried and stored for food or mashed and fermented to make alcoholic beverages.

Octopus Agave is good in large pots or as an accent plant in the landscape. Its flowers are golden yellow and borne on a 10' stalk. This plant performs well in full sun or partial shade. Appearance will remain acceptable in full shade. Hardy to 15F.

Hummingbirds and orioles are attracted to the nectar in Aloe flowers. Rodents will not eat Aloe.

Aloe barbadensis hybrid (at left)

Many *Aloe* species are available. The hardiest do well planted in the landscape in well-drained soil. Others will be most successful in pots protected from frost and sunburn. All are worth the effort.

Plants with bloom stalks range from 6" in height to well over 8'. Flowers are usually yellow, coral, orange or red and occur between January and September. Foliage may be light to dark green with distinctive bands, blotches or edge color.

Aloe are native to southern and eastern Africa.

Aloe barbadensis (A. vera)

Common name	Medicinal Aloe, Aloe Vera
Usual height	3'
Spacing	4'
Bloom	Spring; yellow
Evergreen	Yes, hardy to 25F
Exposure	Full sun / light shade
Soil	Any with good drainage
Propagation	Offset

Stiff, upright, fleshy leaves form striking rosettes which develop into spreading clumps with the addition of numerous offsets. In spring, the 5' yellow flower stalks attract hummingbirds and orioles. The succulent pulp is an effective treatment for burns and other skin injuries.

Aloe barbadensis

Aloe ferox or Tree Aloe matures as a tree-like specimen on a single trunk. This spectacular species carries its heavily-toothed, 2'-long, blue-green leaves to a height of 6' or more.

Aloe ferox

The spikes of the candelabra-shape inflorescence (flowering portion) are on vertical stems. The closed buds are orange and turn to red as they get ready to open. The plant is solitary without pups. Frost protection is needed in colder areas. Hardy to 24F.

Aloe saponaria, African Aloe, forms an attractive groundcover of spiny, star-like rosettes. In spring, orange flower clusters hover about 1' above the foliage. Hardy to 20F.

Anigozanthos flavidus

An Australian native, this plant is named for the resemblance of its flowers to the kangaroo's paw.

Anigozanthos flavidus

Common name	Kangaroo Paw
Usual height	2'
Spacing	2 - 3'
Bloom	Late spring to fall; yellow
Evergreen	Yes, hardy to 25F
Exposure	Full sun/light shade
Soil	Any with good drainage
Propagation	Root division / tissue culture

The Kangaroo Paw, an Australian native, is named for the resemblance of its flowers to the kangaroo's paw. The foliage is grassy, similar to iris.

Hummingbirds are attracted to the flowers which appear on 5' stalks. Hairy, tubular flowers on other species vary in color from yellow to rust-red. Look for the new dwarf hybrids.

Particularly in the desert, Kangaroo Paw performs best where afternoon shade is provided. Use it as an accent.

Anisacanthus quadrifidus var. *wrightii* 'Mexican Flame'™

Common name	'Mexican Flame'
Usual height	5'
Spacing	5'
Bloom	Primarily fall; red-orange
Evergreen	No, tip burn at 20F; hardy to <10F
Exposure	Full sun / light shade
Soil	Any with good drainage
Propagation	Seed / cuttings

Anisacanthus quadrifidus var. *wrightii* 'Mexican Flame'

The delicate, red-orange flowers of 'Mexican Flame' are attractive to hummingbirds. Flowering starts in late summer and lasts until frost. Use the green foliage of 'Mexican Flame' as a background for gray-leafed plants such as *Encelia farinosa* or *Leucophyllum candidum*. To create a riparian effect, combine 'Mexican Flame' with *Muhlenbergia rigens*.

'Mexican Flame' is native to the trans-Pecos region of Texas and northern Mexico.

A. *quadrifidus* var. *brevilobus* 'Mountain Flame'™ is similar, though less lush in appearance.

The delicate, red-orange flowers of the 'Mexican Flame' are attractive to hummingbirds.

Antigonon leptopus

Place Coral Vine in the hottest part of the garden to mitigate reflected heat and enhance the effect of a mini-oasis.

Antigonon leptopus

Common name	Coral Vine, San Miguelito, Queen's Wreath
Usual height	40', needs support
Spacing	15'
Bloom	Summer through fall; deep rose red, white, hot pink
Evergreen	No, hardy to 30F
Exposure	Full sun / light shade
Soil	Any
Propagation	Seed / cuttings

Provided ample water, Coral Vine luxuriates in the excessive summer heat. It can be quite drought-tolerant as well. Large, heart-shaped, rich green leaves contrast nicely with the bright flowers. The most brilliant cultivar is 'Baja Red' which has watermelon-red flowers.

Most of the top dies in winter but will recover quickly once temperatures warm. Native to Baja California and Sonora, Mexico.

Aquilegia chrysantha

Common name	Golden-spurred Columbine
Usual height	3 - 4'
Spacing	2 - 3'
Bloom	Spring through fall; clear yellow
Evergreen	Yes, hardy to <10F
Exposure	Shade
Soil	Damp, cool
Propagation	Seed

Columbine's delicate foliage is similar to Maidenhair Fern and creates a woodland effect. Native to riparian seeps throughout the Southwest, Columbine prefers damp, shady areas which makes it perfect for those difficult shady spots around buildings.

Cut back old stems for rebloom. If allowed to set seed, Columbine will reseed itself in the garden, however, this will reduce bloom.

Good in a mini-oasis, Columbine also performs well in large pots. Stachys and Columbine are often found growing together in their native habitat.

Aquilegia chrysantha

Hummingbirds are attracted to Columbine. Golden-spurred Columbine is one of the showiest species bearing large flowers up to 3" across with slender spurs 2 to 2-1/2" long.

Asclepias subulata

Common name	Desert Milkweed, Ajamete
Usual height	3 - 4'
Spacing	4'
Bloom	Spring through fall; creamy white
Evergreen	Yes, hardy to 20F
Exposure	Full sun
Soil	Well draining
Propagation	Seed

Composed of vertical, gray-green, leafless stems, Desert Milkweed's form is contemporary and architectural. White, star-shaped flowers with black centers appear in flat-topped clusters. Use it as an accent plant.

The tarantula hawk wasp and various butterflies are attracted to the flowers. Desert Milkweed can take full sun and reflected heat. Native to Arizona and Sonora, Mexico.

Asclepias tuberosa, Butterfly Weed, has lush dark-green foliage and bright-orange flowers in midsummer which attract butterflies and hummingbirds. Plants are 3' x 3'. The cultivars 'Gay Butterflies' have flowers ranging from yellow to red.

Butterfly Weed is dormant in winter when foliage dies to the ground. It is not as drought-tolerant as Desert Milkweed and prefers a more acid soil.

Native to the Rio Grande Valley. Hardy to 5F.

Asclepias subulata

Asparagus densiflorus 'Myers'

Common name	'Myers' Asparagus, Foxtail Fern
Usual height	2'
Spacing	2'
Bloom	Spring and fall; insignificant
Evergreen	Yes, hardy to 28F
Exposure	Light shade
Soil	Well drained and mulched
Propagation	Root division

Resembling green foxtails, the upright stems of 'Myers' Asparagus provide textural and sculptural interest. It performs best in light shade whether planted in pots or in the ground. It is slightly less hardy than A. *densiflorus* 'Sprengeri'. Although it can withstand some drought, regular watering is preferred. Use it to enhance a mini-oasis zone.

Baccharis hybrid 'Centennial'

Common name	Desert Broom, 'Centennial'
Usual height	2 - 3'
Spacing	6'
Bloom	Fall; insignificant
Evergreen	Yes, hardy to 15F
Exposure	Full sun
Soil	Any, even with poor drainage
Propagation	Cuttings

A hybrid of B. *pilularis* and B. *sarothroides*, 'Centennial' is female and is produced from cuttings. Bright-green leaves provide a nice contrast for other arid-region plants.

A hardy, mounding groundcover, 'Centennial' is good for erosion control and is resistant to root rot caused by water molds. It withstands extreme desert heat making it is useful in large areas where the height and width are acceptable.

'Centennial' requires deep, infrequent waterings and responds well to nitrogen fertilizer.

Baileya multiradiata

Common name	Desert Marigold
Usual height	1'
Spacing	2'
Bloom	Possible year-round; yellow
Evergreen	Yes, hardy to 10 - 15F
Exposure	Full sun / very light shade
Soil	Any with good drainage
Propagation	Seed

Bright-yellow, daisy-like flowers are held high above the low, gray foliage. With very little supplemental water, Desert Marigold will bloom nearly year-round in the low desert.

Severe drought and hard frost will stop flowering. Hard frost will also reduce foliage to a small rosette.

Asparagus densiflorus 'Myers'

Baileya multiradiata

Desert Marigold is one of the best wildflowers for the low and intermediate desert. Although perennial, the plants are short-lived.

In areas with thin, rocky or caliche soil, *Bahia absinthifolia* will perform better while providing a similar appearance.

Once established, plants will self-sow, but Desert Marigold is never intrusive or problematic. For best results, sow in fall over raked soil and rake in. For faster results, water in and maintain soil moisture until seedlings are 1-1/2 to 2" high. Then water as necessary to maintain plants.

Seeds are available from local botanical gardens. One-gallon plants are available through retail nurseries. Be careful of over-watering. Container plants provide instant effect and also serve as a seed source.

Desert Marigold is native throughout the Southwest below 5,000'.

Baccharis hybrid 'Centennial'

Bougainvillea brasiliensis

Berlandiera lyrata

Look out, chocoholics! The chocolate scent of these yellow flowers is detectable for quite a distance downwind.

Berlandiera lyrata

Common name	Chocolate Flower, Lyre Leaf
Usual height	6 - 12"
Spacing	2 - 3'
Bloom	Warm season; yellow with green eye
Evergreen	Yes, hardy to 10F
Exposure	Full sun / afternoon shade
Soil	Any with good drainage
Propagation	Seed / cuttings

In winter, Chocolate Flower foliage is a low mass. Through the warm season, however, bright-yellow, daisy-like flowers are displayed above the sage-green, lyre-shaped foliage.

The flowers close into green buttons in the afternoon, then reopen in the morning. Too much shade or drought stops flower production.

Native habitat extends from the plains and hills of West Texas across New Mexico, Arizona and Mexico between 4,000' and 5,000'.

Bougainvillea brasiliensis

Common name	Bougainvillea
Usual height	3 - 20'
Spacing	Varies
Bloom	Warm season; red, pink, orange
Evergreen	Only where protected, hardy to 32F
Exposure	Full sun
Soil	Any with good drainage
Propagation	Cuttings

A native of Brazil, Bougainvillea is one of the most outrageously colorful plants available. Both bush and tall-growing varieties come in a wide variety of brilliant colors.

Although frost-tender, it quickly recovers. Bougainvillea thrives on neglect and performs best in the hottest, driest locations. It even seems to appreciate reflected heat from walls and hardscape.

Pruning encourages branching, which may provide more bloom. Do not fertilize as the only result will be foliage growth.

Bougainvillea can be used as a wall covering, a cascading bank cover, or as color in pots. The shrubby variety 'Hawaii' is especially showy with green and yellow variegated foliage and raspberry flowers. See *Sunset Western Garden Book* for descriptions of many other varieties.

Brahea armata

Common name	Mexican Blue Palm
Usual height	40'
Spacing	12' minimum
Bloom	Spring; creamy white
Evergreen	Yes, hardy to 18F
Exposure	Full sun
Soil	Good drainage
Propagation	Seed

This very slow-growing fan palm with silvery-blue fronds comes from central Baja California. Long racemes of creamy-white flowers hang nearly to the ground. Mexican Blue Palm is one of the most beautiful of all palms. All Brahea are drought-tolerant.

Brahea edulis, Guadalupe Palm, is similar to *B. armata* except leaves are light green and flowers are less showy. Both perform well in the desert.

Native to Guadalupe Island off the coast of Baja California, Guadalupe Palm matures at 30' and is hardy to below 20F.

Brahea armata

Caesalpinia mexicana

The primary advantage of the Mexican Bird of Paradise is cold-tolerance.

Caesalpinia gilliesii

Caesalpinia cacalaco, Cascalote, is hard to find but worth the search. It develops into a small tree 15' x 15' with winter flowers, but needs a warm location (above 25F) so the buds do not freeze.

Its rich green foliage shows off the thorny stems with flowers at branch ends. Branches bear thorns similar to roses.

Native to tropical, deciduous forests in Sinaloa, Oaxaca and Vera Cruz, Mexico. Seeds are used to produce a black dye and the wood a red dye. Hardy to 20F.

Caesalpinia gilliesii, Desert Bird of Paradise, has relatively sparse foliage. Flowers are medium yellow with long red stamens. Mature size varies from 5' x 5' to 8' x 8' depending on water availability.

Native to Argentina, the Desert Bird of Paradise is extremely drought-tolerant and cold-hardy to 5-10F.

Caesalpinia mexicana, Mexican Bird of Paradise, bears lush green foliage year-round. Throughout the warm season, lemon-yellow flowers in 6"-long clusters contrast nicely with the abundant green foliage.

Mature height is 8-10' and recommended spacing is 10'. Mexican Bird of Paradise can easily be pruned into a small tree. Plant in full sun to prevent "leggy" growth. It does well in any well-drained soil.

Native to northern Mexico. Hardy to 18F.

Caesalpinia pulcherrima, Red Bird of Paradise, is unequalled in showy summer color. Brilliant red-orange flowers are offset by lush green foliage which may freeze to the ground. Mature size is approximately 6' x 6'.

Native throughout Mexico. Hardy to 30F.

Calliandra californica and C. peninsularis

Common name	Baja-red Fairy Duster
Usual height	5'
Spacing	5'
Bloom	Nearly year-round; red
Evergreen	No, hardy to 26F
Exposure	Full sun / light shade
Soil	Any
Propagation	Seed

Both C. *californica* and C. *peninsularis* and their hybrids are sold in nurseries as Baja-red Fairy Dusters.

C. *californica* is from the central desert of Baja California and is, therefore, the more cold-hardy choice. It has 5-15 pairs of leaflets. C. *peninsularis* is from the warmer cape region and has 18-25 pairs of leaflets.

Both are decorated nearly year-round with bright-red, "shaving-brush" flowers. Naturally, hummingbirds find this attractive.

The finely cut, dark-green foliage may be deciduous in cold areas. It suffers twig and branch dieback at 22F. Baja-red Fairy Duster is suitable for a large pot or as an open shrub in the landscape.

Calliandra eriophylla, known as Fairy Duster, is native to the Sonoran Desert. Primarily a spring bloomer, its flowers may range in color from nearly white to deep rose. A short flowering period in the fall may occur. Fairy Duster grows about 3' high and 4' wide.

Fairy Dusters are drought-tolerant, but need supplemental water in summer. Protect them from rodents when newly planted. Hardy to 0-10F.

Calylophus hartwegii 'Sierra Sundrop'™

Common name	Calylophus
Usual height	2'
Spacing	2 - 3'
Bloom	Spring through fall; lemon yellow
Evergreen	Yes, hardy to 5F
Exposure	Bright light / afternoon shade
Soil	Any
Propagation	Cuttings

Calliandra californica

This primrose relative can provide a spot of color or serve as a groundcover in small areas. Pollinated by moths, the flowers open in early evening and remain open the following day. It is native throughout Texas, New Mexico, Arizona and Mexico at 4,500-7,000'.

It will grow into the base of a loosely branched shrub such as *Salvia microphylla* for a pleasing effect. Calylophus also works well among boulders. Provide supplemental water through the warm season to maintain appearance and extend bloom season. For a smashing effect, plant Calylophus with *Verbena rigida*.

Calylophus hartwegii 'Sierra Sundrop'

Cassia biflora

Botanists have recently divided the genus *Cassia* into three genera: Australian and African species remain in the genus *Cassia*. American species are now either classified as belonging to the genus *Senna* or the genus *Chamaechrista*. Some species names have also been revised. For ease of use, those referenced here are listed by the old species names under *Cassia* with the new botanical names provided in parenthesis.

With careful planning, you can select Cassia for nearly year-round bloom. All Cassia have yellow flowers; most are fragrant. All are good for attracting bees. Depending on the species, they may be evergreen or deciduous and bloom in the spring, summer or fall. Prune each species *after* its flowering period.

Most Cassia grow to 6' in height. Plant them at least 6' apart in full sun. Good drainage is required. They may be propagated from seed or cuttings.

Cassia artemisioides, Feathery Cassia, is the species most commonly planted. Gray, needle-like, evergreen foliage shows off the yellow spring flowers. Native to Australia. Hardy to 15-20F; tip burn may occur at 20F.

Cassia biflora (Senna pallida), Twin-flower or Sonoran Cassia, has dark-green, deciduous foliage. Its long bloom period extends from spring through fall. Native throughout Mexico. Hardy to 25F.

Cassia candolleana, New Zealand Cassia, bears dark-green, evergreen foliage. Fall flowers are golden yellow. This Cassia won't tolerate over-watering. Hardy to 20F.

Cassia goldmanii (Senna polyantha), Goldman's Cassia, is a hard-to-find summer bloomer. New growth is bronze which later turns to green. Foliage is deciduous. It is very slow-growing. Native to southern Baja California. Hardy to 20F.

Cassia nemophila

To ensure flower production, prune Cassia only after its bloom season.

Cassia nemophila, Desert Cassia, is a spring bloomer. Its needle-like foliage is similar to C. *artemisioides* but greener. Native to Australia. Hardy below 19F.

Cassia phyllodenia, Silver-leaf Cassia, blooms from December through April. Sickle-shape, blade-like leaves shimmer in the breeze.

This dense, fast-growing shrub forms an effective screen. The silver foliage is a good backdrop for the red flowers of *Salvia greggii*. Native to Australia. Hardy to 20-22F.

Cassia wislizenii (Senna wislizenii), Shrubby Cassia, has deciduous, dark-green, finely-textured foliage. This Texas native bears large, bright-yellow flower clusters which provide excellent summer color. Although hard to find, it's a real winner. With age, it can become 9' high. The hardiest Cassia available in the nursery industry, it is hardy to 0-5F.

Cassia phyllodenia

Cercidium floridum

Cercidium are kind to allergy sufferers as they are pollinated by bees.

Cercidium floridum, Blue Palo Verde, has blue-green foliage and bark. With age, the bark becomes rough and brown. The foliage is slightly weeping compared to the stiff forms of other Cercidium.

Native to Arizona, Sonora and Baja California. Blue Palo Verde flowers are bright yellow. Mature size is approximately 30' x 30'. Hardy to 10F.

Cercidium microphyllum, Little-leaf or Foothill Palo Verde, is the toughest Palo Verde in the Arizona desert. Mature size is approximately 20' x 20'.

Foliage and bark are often described as lime green. Its flowers are a soft, sulfur yellow and begin about the time the Blue Palo Verde are finished blooming.

Due to its slow growth, few nurseries propagate Little-leaf Palo Verde. Boxed and salvaged native specimens are available. Native to Arizona, Sonora and Baja California. Hardy to 12-15F.

Cercidium praecox, Palo Brea or Sonoran Palo Verde, is a popular "designer tree" which many landscape professionals favor due to its distinctive, angular growth habit.

On maturity, the canopy will be approximately 20' high. When spaced 30' apart, the branch ends overlap. Foliage is semi-evergreen. Palo Brea does well in any sunny location with well-drained soil.

When it blooms in May, all the branches look like yellow rods. The bark remains green, even with age. Some tip damage may occur around 17F. Beware of hybrids which do not have the distinctive growth habit or do not retain the green bark. Native to central Sonora, Mexico and Baja California. Hardy to 20F.

Cercidium floridum

Cercidium praecox

Once established, Cercidium will survive on rainfall in the desert. Blooming Palo Verde are often the subject of artists and photographers.

Cereus hildmannianus

Cereus hildmannianus

Common name	Hildmann's Cereus
Usual height	15'
Spacing	10'
Bloom	Spring through summer; white
Evergreen	Yes, hardy to 24F
Exposure	Full sun / light shade
Soil	Drainage needed
Propagation	Cuttings

Huge white flowers (up to 8") open at night on this, the hardiest Cereus. This variety is the most commonly seen and is readily available. Fast-growing, it quickly provides a strong vertical element in gardens. Native to Brazil.

Chilopsis linearis

Common name	Desert Willow
Usual height	25'
Spacing	15 - 25'
Bloom	Warm season; lavender
Evergreen	No, hardy to 0F
Exposure	Full sun
Soil	Needs good drainage
Propagation	Seed / cuttings

Beautiful in summer, awful in winter: The graceful, willowy foliage and exotic orchid-like flower clusters are irresistible, but in winter, abundant seed pods hang on the branches for a terribly unkempt appearance.

Chilopsis linearis

Desert Willow does best as a background tree. The flower color ranges from nearly white to a showy red-violet. Clusters of trumpet-shaped flowers appear on branch ends. Select plants while in bloom to ensure getting your color preference.

Desert Willow grows in desert washes up to 5,000' elevation throughout the Southwest. Supplemental water is needed only in summer.

Chorisia speciosa (both photos)

Chorisia produce a spectacular fall flower display.

Chorisia speciosa

Common name	Silk-floss Tree
Usual height	30 - 60'
Spacing	30'
Bloom	Fall; pink-wine red
Evergreen	Briefly deciduous, hardy to 26 - 28F
Exposure	Full sun
Soil	Good drainage
Propagation	Seed / cuttings

These green-barked branches are studded with enormous spines. (Chorisia was surely a source of cavemen's clubs.) Native to South America, the young trees need frost protection.

In the fall, all the foliage drops and beautiful lily-like flowers appear. This species offers reliable flower color. It is best used in large sheltered courtyards. Native to Brazil.

Cordia boissieri

Common name	Anacahuita
Usual height	10'
Spacing	10'
Bloom	Warm season; white
Evergreen	Yes, hardy to 22F
Exposure	Full sun, light shade
Soil	Any
Propagation	Seed

Anacahuita is native to the lower Rio Grande Valley of Texas and throughout Mexico. Large, leathery, dark blue-green leaves provide a good backdrop for clusters of 2" white flowers. The appearance is refreshing. Although hardy to 22F, in a sudden freeze the dead leaves will stay on the branches.

Cordia parvifolia, Little-leaf Cordia, is an arching, open shrub. Deciduous and cold-tolerant, it grows 5-6' tall. Clusters of small

Cycas revoluta

white flowers appear through the warm season. Native to Arizona, Sonora and southern Baja California. Hardy to 18F.

Cycas revoluta

Common name	Sago Palm, Cycad
Usual height	Slow to 10'
Spacing	4 - 5'
Bloom	Spring; tan
Evergreen	Yes, hardy to 15F
Exposure	Shade
Soil	Good drainage
Propagation	Seed / offset

Sago Palm is not a palm, but a primitive cone-bearing plant related to conifers. Tan, seed-bearing bracts form on female plants. Male plants produce brown flowers in an interesting cone form in the spring. The common name is from the palm-like foliage. In spite of its delicate appearance, the Sago Palm is extremely tough and somewhat drought-tolerant. It can be acclimated to full sun. Also suitable for large pots.

Sago Palm, a native of southern Japan and Java, provides an exotic influence in shade areas which are difficult to plant in the desert.

Cordia boissieri

Dalea frutescens 'Sierra Negra'

Dalea greggii (around saguaros)

Dalea pulchra

***Dalea frutescens* 'Sierra Negra,'**™ Black Dalea, grows to 3' high x 5' wide in a sunny location with well-drained soil. Airy branches clad with silvery-green foliage bear clusters of rose-purple flowers in late summer and fall.

Light pruning in the spring will produce more compact plants. Cold or drought will cause partial defoliation of this semi-evergreen Chihuahuan Desert native. It is drought-tolerant once established. Native to the trans-Pecos region of Texas. Hardy to 0F.

Dalea greggii, Trailing Indigo Bush, is a spreading groundcover. Purple flowers appear in spring and the bloom persists through the season for Fairy Duster which complements it.

Trailing Indigo blends well with native desert plants. This is one of the hardiest groundcovers. It grows to approximately 1' high x 6' wide. Native to Texas and northern Mexico. Hardy to 0-5F.

Dalea pulchra, Pea Bush, has fine, evergreen foliage which is silvery-gray. Flowering bushes appear smoky when in bloom. Pea Bush is valuable for winter color from November to April when little else is blooming. It is cold- and drought-tolerant.

Plant Pea Bush in full sun where it can mature to 3-4' in height. Space 4-5' apart. Pea Bush needs soil with good drainage.

Pea Bush's gray foliage and red-violet flowers combine well with Encelia and Calliandra.

Native to southeastern Arizona

Dasylirion wheeleri (both photos)

Unlike agave, Desert Spoon usually does not die after blooming.

and northern Mexico from 3,000-5,000'. Hardy to 0F.

Dalea versicolor* var. *sessilis blooms in both spring and fall; flowers are purple. The evergreen foliage matures at 4-5' high and wide. It performs well in either full or filtered sun.

Native at 3,000-5,000' throughout southeastern Arizona and northern Mexico. Hardy to 5F.

Dasylirion wheeleri

Common name	Desert Spoon, Sotol
Usual height	4'
Spacing	6'+
Bloom	Summer; creamy yellow
Evergreen	Yes, hardy to -5 to 0F
Exposure	Full sun, light shade
Soil	Well draining
Propagation	Seed

Slim, blue-green leaves form a spiky hemisphere. Teeth line the leaf edges. The flower spike can be over 10' tall. Plants are either male or female with different flower forms. Desert Spoon is both cold- and drought-hardy. Grow it for form and texture.

Native at 3,000-5,000' throughout Arizona, New Mexico, the trans-Pecos region of Texas and northern Mexico.

D. acrotriche, Green Desert Spoon, is faster-growing with green leaves. Rabbits will eat young plants to the ground. Hardy to 5-10F.

Dietes vegeta

Hop Bush provides a fast-growing dense screen.

Dodonaea viscosa

Dietes bicolor

Common name	Evergreen Iris, Fortnight Lily
Usual height	2'
Spacing	2'
Bloom	Spring and fall; sulfur yellow
Evergreen	Yes, hardy to 13 - 18F
Exposure	Light to medium shade
Soil	Well drained and mulched
Propagation	Root division

Evergreen Iris is good near pools, fountains or in shady areas where a stream bed is simulated. Stiff, iris-like leaves provide textural interest. Flowers resemble a miniature Japanese iris. Remove forming seed pods to extend bloom period, but do not remove flower stalks. Native to South Africa.

D. vegeta has white flowers with purple and yellow markings near the throat. Hardy to 13-18F.

Dodonaea viscosa

Common name	Hop Bush
Usual height	12'
Spacing	10'
Bloom	Spring, insignificant
Evergreen	Yes, hardy to 10F
Exposure	Full sun, very light shade
Soil	Good drainage
Propagation	Cuttings

Cold- and drought-tolerant, this Arizona native is distributed throughout pan-subtropic regions worldwide. Bright-green foliage is coarser than most desert vegetation. Pinkish, papery fruit stands out against the foliage.

Hop Bush provides a fast-growing dense screen and is a good backdrop for shrubs with gray foliage. Don't over-water it.

D. viscosa purpurea, Purple Hop Bush, is less hardy (to 20F) and sensitive to over-watering. Foliage turns plum-color with cool weather.

Dyssodia pentachaeta

Common name	Golden Fleece, Dahlberg Daisy
Usual height	Less than 1'
Spacing	1' plus
Bloom	Warm season; bright yellow
Evergreen	Short-lived perennial or annual, hardy to 10F
Exposure	Full sun
Soil	Sandy, good drainage
Propagation	Seed

Dyssodia pentachaeta

Seed Golden Fleece in place as a wildflower or purchase plants for immediate effect. It fits easily between stepping stones. Bright-green foliage is composed of tiny needle-like leaves. Bright-yellow, daisy flowers persist through the warm season.

Dyssodia needs some supplemental water to keep it going. It readily reseeds. Native to central Arizona, Texas and northern Mexico at 2,500-4,500'.

Golden Barrel Cactus is most attractive in groupings and is suitable for use in large pots.

Echinocactus grusonii

Echinocactus grusonii

Common name	Golden Barrel Cactus
Usual height	2 - 4'
Spacing	3'
Bloom	Spring; yellow
Evergreen	Yes, hardy to <18F
Exposure	Light shade
Soil	Good drainage
Propagation	Seed

Beautiful golden spines make this cactus colorful year-round. Native to southern Mexico, it prefers light shade, but can be acclimated to full sun.

Golden Barrel Cactus is most attractive in groupings and is suitable for use in large pots. Water every two weeks in summer.

Echinocereus engelmannii

Common name	Hedgehog Cactus
Usual height	18"
Spacing	3 - 4'
Bloom	Spring; light pink to fuchsia
Evergreen	Yes, hardy to <18F

Exposure	Full sun to light shade
Soil	Good drainage
Propagation	Seed / cuttings

A Sonoran Desert native, Hedgehog Cactus adds textural interest to native desert landscapes.

Plant size and flower color are diverse. Clumps can become 3' or more in diameter. Flower color may vary from light pink to fuchsia.

Drought- and cold-hardy, Hedgehog Cactus responds to weekly watering and monthly fertilizing through the warm season for greater bloom.

Plants in the desert are protected by law. Only purchase plants with appropriate state tags. Other species can be found at botanical garden sales and specialty cactus nurseries. All have outstanding flowers.

Echinopsis multiplex

Common name	Easter-lily Cactus
Usual height	12"
Spacing	2'
Bloom	Spring and summer; pink, white, or yellow
Evergreen	Yes, hardy to 19 - 24F
Exposure	Light shade
Soil	Good drainage
Propagation	Seed / offset

These globular cacti from Brazil quickly form dense clumps. Mature clumps may produce 20-30 flowers at one time. Large white, pink or yellow flowers open at night throughout the summer. Many are very fragrant.

Water weekly and fertilize monthly during warm season. They are suitable for pots or the ground. Many wonderful hybrids are available at botanical garden plant sales.

Echinocereus engelmannii

The short-lived, exotic flowers of the Echinopsis perfume the night air.

Echinopsis multiplex hybrid Stars & Stripes

Encelia farinosa

Eremophila decipiens

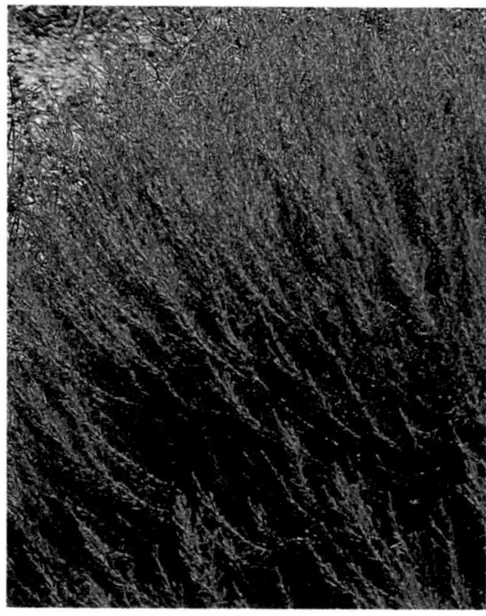

Ericameria laricifolia

Encelia farinosa

Common name	Brittlebush
Usual height	3'
Spacing	4'
Bloom	Early spring; yellow
Evergreen	No, hardy to 26F
Exposure	Full sun
Soil	Good drainage
Propagation	Seed

Native to the Sonoran Desert, Encelia prefers the hottest, sunniest areas. It will freeze in colder locations.

Coarse silvery foliage provides interesting color and texture. Yellow, daisy flowers are held high above the foliage. Shear the spent flowers off for a neater look.

Under natural conditions, Brittlebush is dormant due to drought in summer. Water only to establish and afterward only to maintain appearance. Overwatering produces ungainly growth. Brittlebush is available in gallon containers or can be seeded as a wildflower.

Eremophila decipiens

Common name	Poverty Bush
Usual height	2'
Spacing	3'
Evergreen	Yes, hardy to <19F
Bloom	February to May; red-orange
Exposure	Full sun, light shade
Soil	Good drainage
Propagation	Cuttings

Slender green leaves contrast with bright red-orange flowers. Poverty Bush is suitable for pots or groundcover. Be careful not to over-water in the summer. Native to Australia.

***Eremophila glabra* 'Murchison River'** has gray foliage which is a nice contrast to *Salvia greggii* or *Verbena rigida*. Tubular flowers are orange. Hummingbirds enjoy these Australian natives. Hardy to <21F.

Ericameria laricifolia (Haplopappus laricifolia)

Common name	Turpentine Bush
Usual height	18" - 2'
Spacing	4'
Bloom	Golden yellow
Evergreen	Yes, hardy to 15 - 20F
Exposure	Full sun
Soil	Good drainage
Propagation	Cuttings

In central and southern Arizona and northern Mexico, generally at elevations greater than 3,000', Turpentine Bush is the primary understory plant—similar to Bursage at lower elevations.

Due to the foliage color and texture, it mixes well with other desert vegetation. The bright-green foliage is particularly attractive when placed against grays. The strong scent of the crushed foliage is the source of the name. In fall, golden-yellow flowers cover the top of the plants.

Eucalyptus erythrocorys

Eucalyptus should not be planted in lawns. Over-watering will cause iron chlorosis.

***Eucalyptus erythrocorys*,** Red-cap Gum or Illarie, has sickle-shaped, grass-green leaves which provide interesting texture and good color contrast for other arid-region plants. The vertical form is dominated by a strong central leader.

A square red cap tops each bud capsule, hence the common name. In summer, flowers form in large, lemon-yellow clusters contrasting nicely with the foliage.

Red-cap Gum is good as a street tree or for screening as its foliage provides a good visual block. Mature size is 30' high x 20' wide. Hardy to 28F.

The genus *Eucalyptus* contains hundreds of species which vary from shrubs to enormous trees which are harvested for lumber. Most are native to Australia. To date, only tree forms are available in the southwest. All are grown from seed. They are evergreen and prefer full sun.

Do not allow this plant to dry out in the container. For best results, select small, well-formed plants to avoid getting plants that have become rootbound in the container. Prune any roots encircling the rootball. During planting, be particularly careful with the rootball as Eucalypts are sensitive to root disturbance. The species listed here will generally not cause problems with footings, sidewalks or water lines, as may other species.

Eucalyptus leucoxylon 'Rosea'

Eucalyptus torquata

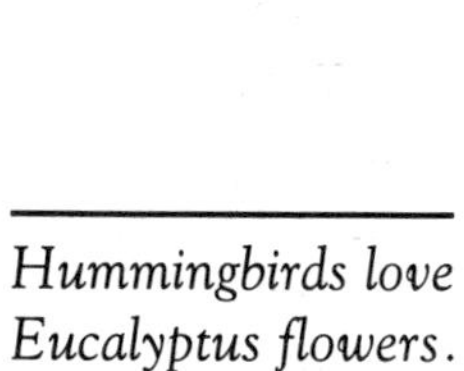

Hummingbirds love Eucalyptus flowers.

Eucalyptus formanii, Forman's Eucalyptus, is a slow-growing, large shrub/small tree. At maturity, both height and width are approximately 15'. The silvery-green, blade-like leaves shimmer in the breeze. In spring, small white flowers appear in frothy clusters. Bark is copper-colored. Hardy to 15F.

***Eucalyptus leucoxylon* 'Rosea,'** White Ironbark, provides fall to winter flower color. It slowly reaches a mature height of 20-30' with a 15-30' spread. This slender, upright tree has blue-green leaves on weeping branches. It is good as a street tree or against buildings.

The flower color and bloom time are variable. This variety has the best flower color. Try to select plants while in bloom. White Ironbark flowers last well in arrangements. Hardy to 14-18F.

Eucalyptus spathulata, Narrow-leaf Gimlet, develops into a beautiful, graceful, multi-trunked canopy tree. The fine, billowy foliage is atypical for Eucalyptus. Its olive and bronze coloring is attractive and blends well with desert plants. The smooth bark is cinnamon-colored. Hardy to 18-26F.

Eucalyptus torquata, Coral Gum, has spring-green new growth with cinnamon-colored branches. Older foliage is blue-green. Bark eventually becomes brown and rough.

Good for cut flowers, the flower color is variable, coral to salmon. Some have more yellow in them. Bloom occurs winter through spring. Coral Gum can be planted in groves. Mature height is 20' with a 15-20' spread. Hardy to 17-21F.

Eucalyptus woodwardii

Eucalyptus woodwardii, Woodward's Black Butt or Lemon-flowered Gum, is an interesting accent tree. The foliage and branches are covered with silver powder. Large and lance-shaped, the leaves are 5" long x 2" wide.

Lemon-flowered Gum is difficult to prune but has an exceptionally long flowering period.

Lemon-flowered Gum grows 30-40' in height with irregular and angular growth habit. Shape it by careful pruning.

Outstanding lemon-yellow flower clusters are produced November through May. These are superb for contemporary or oriental arrangements. Hardy to 17-22F.

Euphorbia myrsinites in bloom

These Euphorbia are tough as nails, withstanding snow, hail and temperatures up to 122F without any visible impact on the foliage. They are also extremely drought-tolerant.

Euphorbia rigida in bloom

Euphorbia rigida

Euphorbia myrsinites (no common name) is even tougher than *E. rigida*, being hardy in all USDA zones to less than -10F. The leaf arrangements on the stems form blue-gray spirals. Overall, this plant is only 6" high x 12" wide. Remove old, yellowing stems after flowering. *E. myrsinites* may be short-lived in warm winter areas. Native to southern Europe.

Euphorbia rigida (E. biglandulosa), a perennial grown for decades, is enjoying a new surge in popularity. Its 2' x 4' blue-gray foliage adds interesting color and texture to the landscape. In spring, branch ends bear broad clusters of glowing, chrome-yellow flowers. To enhance the effect, place the plants where the early morning or late afternoon sun can light them up. Provide full sun and well-drained soil.

After seeds form, the flowering branches decline and need to be removed. *E. rigida* will reseed even in the desert. Plants can be propagated from cuttings. Hardy to 0F.

Ferocactus acanthodes

Ferocactus acanthodes (F. cylindraceus)

Common name	Compass Barrel
Usual height	2 - 4'
Spacing	2 - 4'
Bloom	April - June; yellow-orange
Evergreen	Yes, hardy to 13 - 18F
Exposure	Full sun / light shade
Soil	Well draining
Propagation	Seed

Nearly all Compass Barrels tip to the south or southwest giving them their common name. Skin is dark green, spines rose-red to yellow. Occasionally it will form multiple heads.

Compass Barrel is very cold- and drought-tolerant. Native to the Sonoran Desert.

Ferocactus wislizenii, Fish-hook Barrel, produces flowers July to September which are orange, or red with yellow edges. Curved spines resemble fish hooks.

Native to central Arizona, New Mexico, Texas and northern Mexico at 2,000-4,500'. Hardy to 0F.

Both Compass Barrel and Fish-hook Barrel cacti are protected by state law. Look for appropriate state Department of Agriculture tags attached to the plants. Once the cactus is planted, remove the tags and file them for safekeeping.

Living fences can be made from the thorny branches of the Ocotillo.

Fouquieria splendens, Ocotillo, is a shrub — not a cactus — native to the Sonoran and Chihuahuan Deserts up to 5,000'. At maturity, it may reach 20' x 15' in height and width. Ocotillo is hardy to 0 to 5F. Plant in full sun in soil with good drainage.

Only purchase plants bearing state Department of Agriculture tags as they are protected by state laws.

The leaves drop during drought, thus dormancy depends on available soil moisture. Within three days after a monsoon the Ocotillo will be in full leaf. Its striking form and texture add interest to the landscape. April through May the brilliant red-orange racemes contrast nicely with the Palo Verde and Ironwood blossoms.

Mexicans and Native Americans lash the cane-like branches together to make a coyote fence. If green branches are used, a living fence may develop.

Fouquieria macdougalii, Chunari or Ocotillo Macho, is a fast-growing, tree-like relative of the Ocotillo. It blooms on and off throughout summer.

Chunari is adaptable to large pots. Native to central and southern Sonora, Mexico. Look for it at botanical garden sales. Hardy to 25F.

Fouquieria splendens (both photos)

Fouquieria splendens

Gazania rigens 'Sun Gold'

This morning-glory relative produces masses of huge lavender flowers throughout the hottest part of the summer.

Ipomea carnea var. *fistulosa* (see page 50)

Gazania rigens 'Sun Gold'

Common name	Gazania
Usual height	Less than 1'
Spacing	2'
Bloom	Spring and fall; yellow
Evergreen	Yes, hardy to 20F
Exposure	Full sun / light shade
Soil	Good drainage essential
Propagation	Seed / cuttings

Dazzling daisy flowers adorn this perennial groundcover in spring and fall with intermittent bloom through the summer. This variety seems to perform better than others in the desert.

These African natives are also available in exotic hybrids which can have intricate coloration including eyes, bands or stripes. Colors range from creamy white to rust, rose, yellow and orange.

Particularly in summer, be careful of over-watering. Drip irrigation is better than sprays because it doesn't get the dense foliage wet and allows the soil to dry out between irrigations.

Hesperaloe parviflora (both photos)

Hesperaloe funifera, Coahuilan Hesperaloe, is much larger than *H. parviflora*. The sharp-tipped leaves may reach 4-6' in height, so plant it away from walks. The flower spike is 10' plus with white flowers.

This species and the one following are hard to find but make superbly interesting garden accents. Native to Coahuila, Mexico. Hardy to 5-10F.

Hesperaloe nocturna, Night-flowering Hesperaloe, has white flowers which open at night for pollination by moths. Leaves are 3-4' long with curling white fibers along the margins. Native to central Sonora, Mexico. Hardy to 10-15F.

Hesperaloe parviflora, Red Yucca, grows 2-3' high forming broad clumps. Plant 3' apart in full sun. Coral blooms occur on tall stalks from spring through fall.

Hesperaloe are tough, drought- and cold-hardy accent plants from the Chihuahuan Desert. Their blooms attract moths and hummingbirds. Rodents do not bother them.

This Agave relative is an attractive and hardy accent plant. The flower spike appears in early spring and continues to grow and flower through the fall. The spike can reach 8' plus in height, so don't plant Red Yucca beneath low-branching trees. Leaves are narrow and blue-green. It is suitable for large pots. Hummingbirds can't resist the flowers.

Red Yucca's native habitat is limited to the lower trans-Pecos region of Texas and northern Mexico.

Red Yucca is hardy from 0 to 5F and tolerates any soil.

Justicia californica

Ipomea carnea var. *fistulosa*

Common name	Diez en la Mañana (Ten in the Morning)
Usual height	4 - 10'
Spacing	6'+
Bloom	Summer through fall; lavender
Evergreen	No, hardy to 30F
Exposure	Full sun
Soil	Good drainage
Propagation	Seed

"Diez en la Mañana" refers to the time of day the flowers close in summer. Although the large leaves and flowers look tropical, it dislikes over-watering.

It is most often found in barrios growing and blooming in spite of harsh conditions. If you see one, ask the owner for some seeds.

Plant in a sunny location in spring or early summer so it can be established before winter. Over-watering causes chlorosis. After first frost, cut back branches to 1' above ground.

Native to tropical North and South America.

Justicia californica

Common name	Chuparosa
Usual height	4 - 6'
Spacing	6'
Bloom	Early spring and fall; red-orange
Evergreen	Yes, hardy to 28F
Exposure	Full sun / partial shade
Soil	Well draining
Propagation	Seed / cuttings

Another Sonoran Desert native, Chuparosa is nearly leafless. Stems and leaves are blue-green. From February to May and again in the fall, its showy, red-orange, tubular flowers attract hummingbirds. The flowers have a cucumber flavor and may be used for color and flavor accent in salads.

Although it may suffer frost damage, Chuparosa will quickly regrow when the weather warms. It is usually found growing along washes and needs supplemental water in landscapes to maintain appearance.

Justicia spicigera, Mexican Honeysuckle, is a leafier relative of *J. californica* which performs well in light shade but tolerates full sun and reflected heat.

The velvety leaves are sage-green. In early spring it is covered with fluorescent-orange flowers which persist sporadically through the warm season. It spreads by stolons and can be kept to 2-3' in height. Native to Mexico. With protection from an overhang, it is hardy to 19F.

Lantana

Common name	Lantana
Usual height	1 - 6'
Spacing	4 - 6'
Bloom	Warm season
Evergreen	Yes in protected areas, hardy to 30F
Exposure	Full sun
Soil	Any
Propagation	Seed / cuttings

Three types of Lantana are available in nurseries:
L. camara hybrids grow approximately 2-5' high and wide. Flower clusters may be pure white, orange, yellow or blends of colors such as yellow, pink and purple. They are native to the Carribean.

L. montevidensis, Trailing Lantana, grows 1 to 1-1/2' high x 4-6' wide. The hardiest of the bunch, it produces abundant clusters of lavender flowers and is useful as a groundcover in hot, sunny areas. *L. montevidensis* is native to Uruguay.

Larrea divaricata

Underused as a landscape plant, Creosote is the most common shrub found in the American deserts.

Hybrids between *L. camara* and *L. montevidensis* tend to be relatively low, spreading 2-3' high x 6-8' wide. Colors are yellow or orange. See *Sunset Western Garden Book* for hybrid descriptions.

Because they are frost-tender, it is best to plant Lantana in spring through midsummer so the plants will be established prior to frost. Lantana may freeze to the ground with the first frost. Leave frozen foliage on the plant until the danger of frost is past sometime in April. Although this is unsightly, it will protect the roots.

Butterflies and hummingbirds are attracted to the flowers.

Larrea divaricata (L. tridentata)

Common name	Creosote Bush
Usual height	4 - 8'
Spacing	6 - 8'
Bloom	Warm season after rains; yellow
Evergreen	Yes, hardy to 0 - 5F
Exposure	Full sun
Soil	Any
Propagation	Seed / transplants

Small, bright, olive-green leaves contrast nicely with light-gray bark. The branch structure is very graceful. Night lighting will enhance the sculptural quality of this open shrub. Creosote is native to all deserts in the U.S.

Showy yellow flowers are followed by furry white fruit which contains the seeds. Volatile oils in the leaves are pleasantly fragrant after rain. This is the inspiration for the title of the book, *The Desert Smells Like Rain*, by Gary Paul Nabham (published by Farrar, Straus & Giroux, Inc.).

Creosote is extremely cold- and drought-tolerant. It is available in 1- and 5-gallon containers or in box sizes as native salvaged specimens.

Lantana montevidensis

The Golden Ball Lead Tree is native to the trans-Pecos region, particularly the Big Bend area, of west Texas.

Leucaena retusa

Leucaena retusa

Common name	Golden Ball Lead Tree
Usual height	20'
Spacing	20'
Bloom	Spring; yellow-gold
Evergreen	Semi, hardy to 10F
Exposure	Full sun
Soil	Any
Propagation	Seed

Native to the trans-Pecos region of Texas and northern Mexico, the Golden Ball Lead Tree is a good slow-growing ornamental tree. It bears an abundance of 3/4" round puffball flowers that hang on short stems.

Upon drying, the seed pods drop to the ground. The lacy, medium-green foliage has an interesting texture. The overall form is upright.

Golden Ball Lead Tree is cold- and drought-tolerant. It needs supplemental watering for best performance.

Leucophyllum candidum 'Thunder Cloud'

> *Leucophyllum* is a diverse genus of hardy shrubs from the Chihuahuan Desert. All are cold- and drought-tolerant and primarily reliant on the summer monsoons to induce flowering. Some species will bloom nearly any time the humidity is up.
>
> For many years, *Leucophyllum frutescens*, Texas Sage, has been a landscape staple. Lately, several new species and selections have been collected from the wild and introduced to the landscape industry. Through a breeding program conducted at Texas A&M University, several new cultivars have been developed. The resulting plants are trademarked. Nurseries propagating trademarked plants attach a special identification tag to each plant and pay royalties to Texas A&M. This helps support the program for development of additional plants for landscapes.

***Leucophyllum candidum* 'Silver Cloud,'™** Silver Cloud Sage, gets its name from its fine silvery-white foliage which contrasts nicely with the purple flowers. At maturity, Silver Cloud is approximately 4-5' high x 4-5' wide but can be kept to 2-3'. Use 4' spacing for a continuous mass. Hardy to 5-10F.

***L. candidum* 'Thunder Cloud,'™** Thunder Cloud Sage, is a selection with exceptionally dark-purple flowers whose buds appear black. Mature size is smaller than the species. The silver foliage is a good contrast to groundcovers and larger shrubs with green or coarser foliage. Both are trademarked by Texas A&M. Hardy to 5-10F.

***Leucophyllum frutescens*,** Texas Sage or Cenizo, an old standby, is still reliable. Growing to approximately 6' high x 6' wide, its gray foliage contrasts nicely with other colors and textures. It can become a rangy screening shrub. Pruning will improve its form. Flowers are lavender-pink. Hardy to 5-10F.

***L. frutescens compacta*,** Compact Texas Sage, stays neater. By nature it is more manageable at 4-5' high. Hardy to 5-10F.

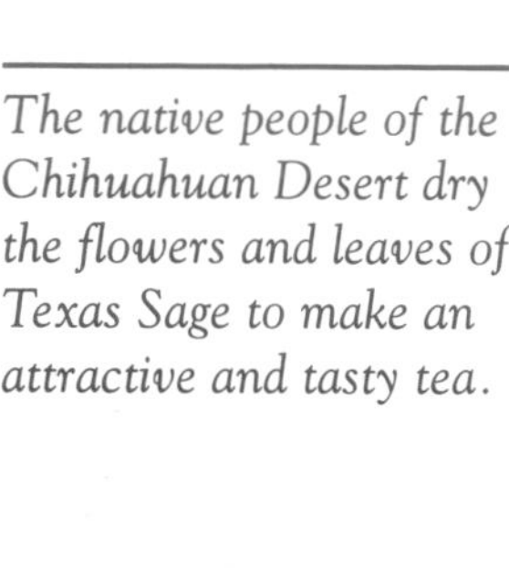

The native people of the Chihuahuan Desert dry the flowers and leaves of Texas Sage to make an attractive and tasty tea.

Leucophyllum frutescens

L. frutescens **'Green Cloud,'™** Green Cloud Sage, has beautiful sage-green foliage which is quite attractive when mixed with the species.

Its mature size is similar to *L. frutescens* although the appearance is neater. With age, it develops a vertical growth habit. Flowers are red-violet. Hardy to 5-10F.

L. frutescens **'White Cloud,'™** White Cloud Sage, has gray foliage and white flowers. This nearly monochromatic coloring can be difficult to use effectively. Best results are achieved by providing a simple darker backdrop such as a wall. Hardy to 5-10F.

Leucophyllum laevigatum, Chihuahuan Sage, offers interesting form, texture and color. The upright branches are clothed with small blue-green leaves which expose the structure.

The Chihuahuan Sage is less reliant on the monsoons than the others for flowering. Even deep irrigation may trigger bloom.

Like the leaves, the fragrant flowers cling tightly to the branches forming lavender rods. Place Chihuahuan Sage where outdoor living areas will be enchanced by the light fragrance.

Mature size is approximately 5' high x 6' wide. Hardy to 10-15F.

***Leucophyllum langmaniae* 'Rio Bravo,'™** Rio Bravo Sage, has foliage that is green like 'Green Cloud,' but smaller. Mature size is smaller also 4-5' high x 4-5' wide, forming a rounded shrub. The large blue flowers open wider than other species. Hardy to 5-10F.

***Leucophyllum pruinosum* 'Sierra Bouquet,'™** Sierra Bouquet Sage, has curled gray foliage and fragrant grape-scented flowers. The large bell-like flowers are periwinkle with white stamens. Mature size is 6' x 6'. Hardy to 5-10F.

Leucophyllum hybrid 'Rain Cloud,'™ Rain Cloud Sage, is a hybrid resulting from a cross between *L. minus* and *L. frutescens*. The foliage resembles *L. frutescens* while the flowers are the typical blue-violet of *L. minus*.

Leucophyllum frutescens 'Green Cloud'

Leucophyllum laevigatum

The red-violet flowers of the Green Cloud Sage are beautiful against the soft-green foliage. This is a great background shrub.

Leucophyllum laevigatum

Chihuahuan Sage tastes as good as it smells.

The growth habit is more vertical than any other Leucophyllum.

Although multiple flowerings are possible, usually only one major display occurs during the season. Alkaline, well-drained soil is essential. Rain Cloud is hardy to 5-10F.

***Leucophyllum zygophyllum* 'Blue Ranger,'** matures at 2-3' high x 3' wide. Angular branches support small green leaves. Blue-violet flowers form a solid mass over the plant. Hardy to 5-10F.

Lophocereus schottii forma monstrosus

Common name	Totem Pole Cactus
Usual height	10'
Spacing	10'
Evergreen	Yes, hardy to 19 - 24F
Bloom	Late spring; pink
Exposure	Full sun
Soil	Good drainage
Propagation	Cuttings

Particularly interesting for its sculptural quality, the Totem Pole's knobby, irregular, medium-green stems are the monstrose (deformed) version of Senita. This slow-growing cactus is spineless. Flowers are insignificant. Plant Totem Pole in groups of two to five plants.

Lophocereus schottii forma monstrosus

Totem Pole is native to southwestern Arizona, and to Sonora and Baja California, Mexico

Lotus rigidus

Common name	Deer Vetch
Usual height	16" - 3'
Spacing	2 - 3'
Bloom	Spring; yellow
Evergreen	No, hardy to 18F
Exposure	Full sun
Soil	Any with drainage
Propagation	Seed / cuttings

This native to the Arizona Upland and chaparral does not do well in clay soils. Deer Vetch bears small, yellow, pea-shaped flowers in spring.

The open blue-green foliage provides interesting texture making Deer Vetch a good contrast for plants with gray foliage. With drought, the leaves fall, leaving the green stems bare. Don't over-water it in summer.

Lotus rigidus

Lysiloma microphyllum

Lysiloma microphyllum* var. *thornberi

Common name	Desert Fern, Feather Bush
Usual height	12 - 15'
Spacing	12'+
Bloom	Spring; white
Evergreen	No, hardy to 22 - 24F
Exposure	Full sun
Soil	Any
Propagation	Seed

Desert Fern is one of the most graceful and cool-looking of the desert plants, a greatly underused Arizona native.

Native to the Rincon Mountains east of Tucson, Arizona and to northern Sonora, Mexico, Desert Fern is drought-tolerant once established. Eventually, it matures into a small tree.

The finely-cut leaves appear lush giving good texture in a mini-oasis. The flowers are small white puffballs. Desert Fern is evergreen in warm, protected areas.

Macfadyena unguis-cati

Common name	Cat's-claw Vine
Usual height	20 - 30'
Spacing	15'
Bloom	Spring; yellow
Evergreen	Mostly, hardy to 13 - 18F
Exposure	Full sun / light shade
Soil	Any
Propagation	Seed

Cat's-claw Vine loves heat—even heat that is reflected off walls and walks. It is named for the claw-like tendrils by which it climbs. Bright-yellow, 2" trumpet flowers contrast with green foliage. Lower branches, which tend to be leafless, develop interesting character with age.

This plant provides fast cover for walls or shade structures. To prevent the wind from blowing it off house walls, provide ties near the top. Native to South America.

Macfadyena unguis-cati

Mascagnia lilacina,
Lavender Orchid Vine, is more hardy than M. *macroptera*, going deciduous but not showing injury at 22F and below. The tiny lavender flowers are abundant when the vine is fertilized. This plant is widely distributed throughout Mexico. Hardy to 15-18F.

Mascagnia macroptera,
Yellow Orchid Vine, is native throughout most of Mexico. This fast-growing, deciduous vine recovers quickly from frost damage. In summer, bright-yellow, orchid-like flower clusters stand out against the green foliage.

Flowers are followed by large yellow-green fruit which are more conspicuous than the flowers.

Mascagnia likes full sun. Mature height is 15-20'. They perform well in any soil. Hardy to 22-24F.

Mascagnia macroptera

Mascagnia love the heat and perform best in protected areas. They need to be attached to walls, but are self-twining on trellises.

Merremia aurea

The cheerful daisies to the right smell like honey.

Melampodium leucanthum

Melampodium leucanthum

Common name	Blackfoot Daisy
Usual height	1'
Spacing	2'
Bloom	Warm season; white with yellow center
Evergreen	Yes, hardy to -5 to 0F
Exposure	Full sun / light shade
Soil	Well drained
Propagation	Seed

Blackfoot Daisy is native to many areas of the Southwest. It is both cold- and drought-hardy.

With supplemental water and a little fertilizer, it will bloom nearly all year. When used in raised planters or pots, the plant oozes over the edge like foam. Well-drained soil is essential. Plant it as groundcover in small areas. Be careful not to over-water.

Merremia aurea

Common name	Yellow Morning Glory Vine, Yuca
Usual height	15'
Spacing	10'
Bloom	Summer; yellow
Evergreen	No, hardy to 26F, dies to ground
Exposure	Full sun
Soil	Any
Propagation	Seed

Yellow Morning Glory is a fast-growing, drought-tolerant vine with dark-green foliage. Large golden-yellow flowers nearly cover the branches.

Tie it to walls or to a trellis. Merremia can be cut back to the ground every year as it grows from a tuber. Native to southe- Baja California.

Clockwise from top left: Mesquite, Creosote and *Muhlenbergia rigens* in foreground.

Muhlenbergia dumosa, Bamboo Muhly, grows to approximately 4' in height and resembles a short bamboo. It is taller and slimmer than Deer Grass. Although evergreen in Phoenix, it may become brown in winter in colder areas.

Use Bamboo Muhly to enhance the effect of the mini-oasis or riparian areas. Native to southern Arizona and northwestern Mexico. Hardy to 20F.

Muhlenbergia emersleyi, Bull Grass, has broader bright-green foliage and bears a creamy, airy inflorescence (flower cluster) in the fall. It matures to 4-5' height and width. Native to Arizona, New Mexico and Texas. Hardy to 5-10F.

Muhlenbergia lindheimeri, Lindheimer Muhly, may become 2-5' in height and width. In the fall, transparent, silvery plumes form graceful arches above the narrow blue-green foliage. Hardy to 5-10F.

Muhlenbergias provide textural interest in the garden. They are native from Texas to California and into northern Mexico at 2,500-7,000'. Because they are Southwestern natives, Muhlenbergias are not likely to become problematic and overtake an area the way some exotic grasses have been known to do when introduced into American landscapes. They are also familiar to wildlife.

Muhlenbergias are evergreen and normally reach 3-4' in height. Plant 4' or more apart in full sun or light shade in well-drained soil.

Muhlenbergia rigens, Deer Grass is a perennial bunch grass native to much of the southwestern United States. It stays green year-round in the Phoenix area. Brown flower/seed heads stand above the foliage and resemble miniature cattails. This is an excellent, soft accent. Hardy to 15F.

Muhlenbergia emersleyi

Myoporum parvifolium

Myoporum is a good replacement for grass where cover is used for eye appeal only.

Myoporum parvifolium

Common name	Prostrate Myoporum
Usual height	1'
Spacing	6 - 8'
Bloom	Spring; white
Evergreen	Yes, hardy to 24F
Exposure	Full sun / light shade
Soil	Any with good drainage
Propagation	Cuttings

Myoporum is grass green and spreads out in an even mat, gracefully flowing over contours. Small, white star-like flowers appear April to May. They turn brown and are unattractive for a short time when viewed closely. Careful water management is essential for long-term success.

Myoporum likes deep waterings every 4-6 days in summer. Use drip irrigation to keep excess water off foliage and minimize bacterial and fungal infections. In winter, overspray from lawn may cause frost damage. Native to Australia.

Nandina domestica

Nandina domestica

Common name	Heavenly Bamboo
Usual height	4 - 6'
Spacing	4'
Bloom	Spring; white
Evergreen	Yes, hardy to 5 - 10F
Exposure	Light shade
Soil	Any except caliche
Propagation	Seed / cuttings / division

Nandina domestica, hardy to 10F, prefers a location with light shade. Its attractive foliage enhances the effect of a mini-oasis. New foliage is bronze, turning green with maturity. Loose clusters of white flowers produce red berries which remain on the plant for quite a while. Cold weather brings out purple, bronze and crimson.

Nandina is a native of China and Japan.

N. domestica 'compacta' is lower-growing (4-5') with lacier foliage than the species.

N. domestica 'nana' is typical of several very dwarf (1'- high) varieties which can be used as a clumpy low groundcover or as a solitary color accent. It is hardy to 5-10F.

See *Sunset Western Garden Book* for descriptions of additional varieties.

Nerium oleander 'Petite Salmon'

Nerium oleander

Hardy, reliable, evergreen and colorful, Oleander is one of the most useful landscape shrubs. Tall-growing varieties are quite wide and dense, so give them plenty of room. Their roots are aggressive; don't plant near a sewer line or septic system. They recover quickly from frost damage.

Select large varieties while in bloom. All varieties bloom through the warm season. Colors range from white to pink to red with various shades in between.

With work, Oleander can be trained into an attractive single or multi-trunk tree. The larger-sized varieties may mature at 12'-20' high and wide depending on the variety. Hardy to 20F. Native to the Mediterranean.

N. oleander 'Little Red' has dark-red flowers and blooms less than others. Mature height is 5-8'. Hardy to 20F.

N. oleander 'Mrs. Roeding' grows 6-8' high x 10' wide. Flowers are double and coral. This is an excellent selection for use where lower screening is needed. Allow room for its natural mature size and you will never have to prune it. Hardy to 20F.

N. oleander 'Petite Pink' and 'Petite Salmon' can be kept at 3-6'. 'Petite Salmon' is somewhat more floriferous than the 'Petite Pink'. Hardy to 26F.

Oleander plant parts are poisonous if eaten. Even the milky sap can irritate skin. Do not inhale its smoke or use the wood for barbecue. Rabbits and deer leave it alone.

Oenothera caespitosa

Oenothera berlandieri

Oenothera stubbii

Oenothera berlandieri

Common name	Mexican Evening Primrose
Usual height	12 - 18"
Spacing	3'
Bloom	Warm season; pink
Evergreen	Mostly, hardy to 24F
Exposure	Full sun / light shade
Soil	Any
Propagation	Cuttings

This hardy groundcover spreads by root sprouts, making it good for erosion control once established. It is native to East Texas and Mexico.

Pink flowers cover the plant in spring. Sporadic flowering continues through the warm season. It needs adequate water to remain attractive.

In cold weather the leaves turn red. Exceptional cold will freeze it to ground. New growth will appear with warm weather. Cut it back with a Weedeater™ if growth gets rangy.

Mexican Primrose's only real pest is the flea beetle which has a shiny, metallic, dark blue-green back. Flea beetles can invade and devour the foliage in a very short time. Watch for damage in early spring and spray immediately with an insecticide such as Diazinon.™ Insects may return in the fall.

Oenothera caespitosa, White Evening Primrose, is a beautiful native of the Southwest. Long, narrow, soft blue-green leaves form attractive rosettes.

Throughout the warm season, large 2" white flowers open in early evening and stay open until mid-morning. Although sometimes hard to find, White Evening Primrose is quite rewarding. Hardy to 10F.

Oenothera stubbii, Saltillo Primrose, has long, narrow, green foliage which forms rosettes. Large, 2" yellow flowers open at dusk.

Sprays of new growth spring from old rosettes resembling a punk hairdo. Branch ends root where new growth touches the

Olneya tesota (also upper right corner photo)

ground. The root forms a large white tuber which increases drought-tolerance. It may be hard to find. Native to Coahuila, Mexico. Hardy to 18-20F.

Olneya tesota

Common name	Desert Ironwood
Usual height	20 - 30'
Spacing	30'+
Bloom	May; lavender
Evergreen	No, hardy to 20 - 22F
Exposure	Full sun
Soil	Any
Propagation	Seed

Desert Ironwood, native to the Sonoran Desert, is rarely available as large nursery stock because it is extremely slow-growing. Beautiful specimens salvaged from the desert in areas of new development are available from some specialty nurseries.

Ironwood develops interesting gnarly trunks. Best used as a visual focus, these trees are expensive, but worth the price as one tree can make the landscape.

Dormancy may be caused either by severe frost or drought. The gray-green leaves fall in late spring just as bloom starts. Summer monsoons trigger a new flush of foliage. Medium-gray bark becomes rough with age.

Olneya tesota (salvaged)

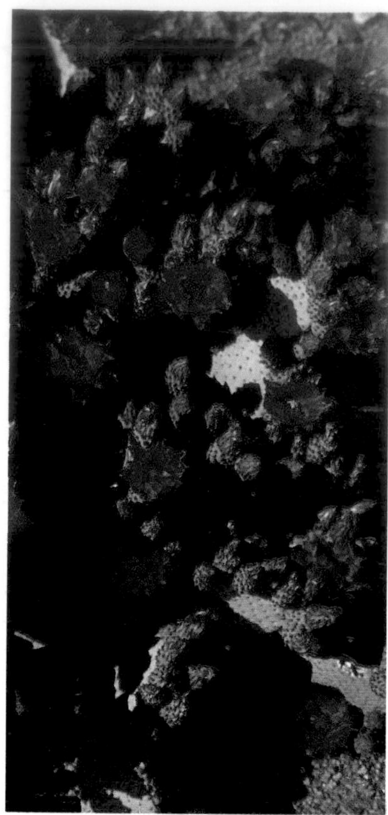

Opuntia basilaris

Opuntia acanthocarpa

O*puntia* can be divided into two general categories: those with flat stems, called *prickly pear*, and those with cylindrical stems, called *cholla*. Some Opuntia have large spines. All have small, splinter-like spines — called *glochids* — which can be a major hazard.

Prior to transplanting or pruning, dampen Opuntia with a gentle spray of water to keep the glochids from blowing around. A hard spray may blow them into your eyes. To remove glochids from small areas of your skin, use tape. On larger areas, pour on white glue, allow to partially harden then peel off. Body hair will be removed, but so will the glochids.

Opuntia acanthocarpa, Buckhorn Cholla, covers large areas of the Sonoran Desert. It is similar to Staghorn Cholla from the southern part of Arizona. Flower color is variable — yellow, orange or rose. Flower buds are harvested by Native Americans and dried for food. This cholla matures at 3-5' in height. Hardy to 19-24F.

Opuntia basilaris, Beavertail Prickly Pear, forms a low-growing groundcover of light blue-green pads. Fuchsia blooms appear in early spring. Native to the Mojave Desert. Hardy to 10F.

Opuntia ficus-indica, Indian Fig, is a tree-form prickly pear from central Mexico. The large fruit is quite tasty. Mature height may be 8-10'. Hardy to 20F.

Opuntia phaeacantha (fruit)

Opuntia phaeacantha (flowers with brittlebush)

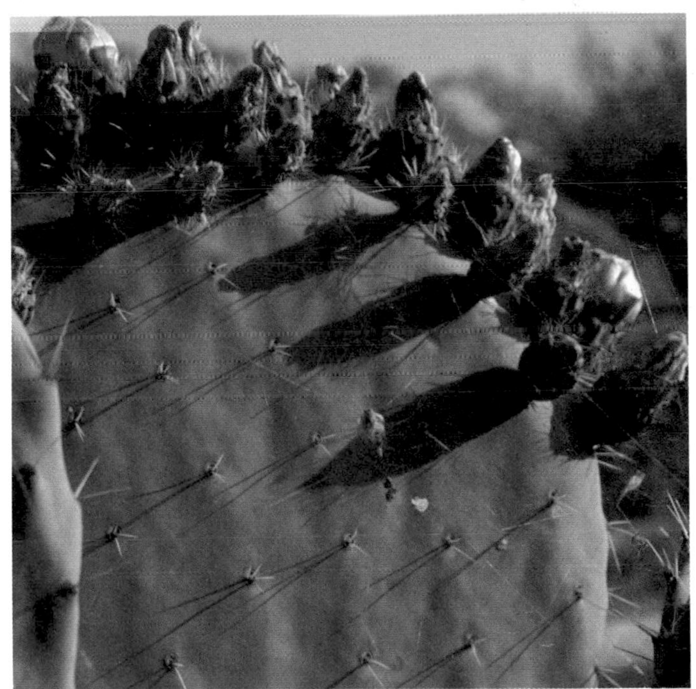

Opuntia robusta

Opuntia leptocaulis, Desert Christmas Cholla, is a small (3-4"-high) cane-type cholla with abundant small, red fruits which persist through winter. Good for landscape interest. Native to the Sonoran Desert. Hardy to 0F.

Opuntia phaeacantha var. discata (O. engelmannii), Engelmann's Prickly Pear, is a native of the Sonoran and Chihuahuan Deserts. Light-green pads support clear yellow flowers followed by dark red fruit. Native Americans gather the fruit to use as both a food and dye. Hardy to 10F.

Opuntia robusta is the most beautiful of the tree prickly pear. Its 12"-diameter, pale-blue pads are almost perfectly round. Maturing at 10' x 10', it is a moderate grower.

Large, clear-yellow flowers grace the upper edge of the pads in spring. The fruit is large (nearly fist-sized) and sweet. Pollination from a different clone is needed. Native to the southern Chihuahuan Desert. Hardy to less than 15F.

Opuntia violacea santa-rita (both photos)

Young prickly pear pads may be peeled, cooked and used in salads or salsa. Peeled raw pads may also be used as a poultice on injuries.

Opuntia violacea santa-rita

Common name	Purple Prickly Pear
Usual height	3'
Spacing	4'+
Bloom	April and May; yellow
Evergreen	Yes, hardy to 15F
Exposure	Full sun
Soil	Any
Propagation	Cuttings

Native to the Santa Rita Mountains near Tucson, this prickly pear is particularly colorful. Cold weather brings out the purple in the pads. Select plants in winter for best pad color. Clear, yellow flowers appear while pad color is strong. There are many variations, some nearly spineless, others with long spines.

Pachycereus marginatus
(Stenocereus marginatus)

Common name	Mexican Organ Pipe
Usual height	10'
Spacing	10'
Bloom	Late spring; pink
Evergreen	Yes, hardy to 20F
Exposure	Full sun
Soil	Any with drainage
Propagation	Cuttings

Giant cucumber-like stems make this is a bold and dramatic accent plant. It is composed of dark-green skin with white ribs of areoles; showy against a wall.

Mexican Organ Pipe is fast-growing for a cactus. Additional stems sprout from the base. Native to southern Mexico.

This plant is being researched as a source for a skin-cancer treatment.

Pachycereus marginatus

Mexicans lash Mexican Organ Pipe cuttings together and use them as fences.

Penstemon eatonii

Penstemon parryi

P*enstemon* is a beautiful, wide-ranging American wildflower also known as Beardtongue. Plants are perennial with sparse low-growing foliage 1-3' high which is not noticeable most of the year. In spring and summer, tall 2-6' high flower stalks grow high above the plants bearing flowers of red, pink, purple, blue or white. When several species are planted together, the show is outstanding. Hummingbirds can't resist the flowers.

Plant 2-3' apart in full sun or light shade in soil with good drainage. Don't over-water during summer. Provide afternoon shade in the desert. Penstemon can be propagated by seed or cuttings.

***Penstemon baccharifolius* 'Del Rio,'**™ Rock Penstemon, is shrubbier than most. Leaves are dark-green and roundish with a serrated edge. Small, tubular, scarlet flowers are borne on short stems just above the foliage throughout summer. Mature size is approximately 2' x 2'. Native to the trans-Pecos region of Texas. Hardy to 5F.

Penstemon barbatus, Scarlet Bugler, blooms in summer. Scarlet flowers are displayed on 2' stalks above the green foliage. Native at 4,000-10,000' in northern Arizona and central highlands of Mexico. Hardy to 0F.

Penstemon eatonii, Firecracker Penstemon, has scarlet flowers and large, triangular leaves. Native at 2,000-7,000' in northern and central Arizona. Hardy to 10-15F.

Penstemon fendleri, Fendler's Penstemon, has foliage similar to *P. parryi* but smaller (1' x1') and 3' flower stalks which bear

Penstemon pseudospectabilis

lavender blossoms in late spring. Native at 4,000-5,000' in southeastern Arizona, Texas and northern Mexico. Hardy to 0F.

Penstemon palmeri, Palmer's Penstemon, has powdery blue-green leaves with serrated edges which are fused around the stems. Flowers are large (1-1/2") and fragrant. Color may range from white to soft pink-lavender. Mature height is 4-6'. Native at 3,500- 6,500' in Utah, Arizona and California. Hardy to 0F.

Penstemon parryi, Parry's Penstemon, has hot-pink flowers on 3-5' stalks. Foliage is limited to a basal rosette. Native at 1,500-5,000' in central and southern Arizona and in Sonora, Mexico. Hardy to 15F.

Penstemon pseudospectabilis, Canyon Penstemon, has fuchsia-colored flowers on 3-4' stalks. Triangular leaves are blue-green with serrated edges fused around the stems. Native at 2,000-7,000' from southwestern New Mexico to eastern California. Hardy to 10F.

Penstemon spectabilis, Royal Penstemon, has foliage similar to *P. pseudospectabilis* and "litmus-paper" blue-purple flowers on 3' spikes. Native below 6,000' in coastal California to northern Baja California. Hardy to 10-15F.

Penstemon superbus, Superb Penstemon, has dark-coral flowers on 3-4' stalks. Foliage is dark blue-green, stalk is dark rose. Native to southeastern Arizona and Chihuahua, Mexico at 4,500-5,000'. Hardy to 5-10F.

Penstemon thurberi, Thurber's Penstemon, forms a rounded bush 18" x 18". Delicate green leaves contribute to its airy appearance. Small lavender flowers appear in late spring and summer. Spreads by stolons. Native to southeastern Arizona, New Mexico and Baja California at 2,000-5,000'. Hardy to 5-10F.

Penstemon wrightii, Wright's Penstemon, is native to the Big Bend region. Egg-shaped light-green leaves are larger (2-3") than most Penstemon foliage. Mature height is 2-3'. The 1" flowers are pink-rose. Blooms appear spring through fall. Hardy to 5-10F.

Penstemon superbus

Phoenix dactylifera

Phoenix dactylifera

Common name	Date Palm
Usual height	40 - 80'
Spacing	15 - 20' minimum
Bloom	Summer
Evergreen	Yes, hardy to 15F
Exposure	Full sun
Soil	Any with good drainage
Propagation	Seed / offset

The feather-type fronds of the Date Palm are gray-green. Leaflets are stiff with sharp points — a hazard on short trees. Remove suckers from the base to maintain a single trunk. Avoid severely pruning the fronds as this will stress the plant.

Rock squirrels will climb the trunk and steal the fruit, which can be messy. Hand pollination and protective bags are necessary for good-quality fruit. Contact your local agricultural extension service for proper technique.

Date Palm's classic form is popular in landscapes. It is native to Arabia and North Africa.

Phoenix roebelenii, Pigmy Date Palm, is a graceful, multi-trunk, slow-growing palm. It can be used in large pots or planted in the ground in protected areas. Fronds are rich green.

Full or light shade is preferred, although plants can be acclimated to full sun. Native in Assam, India to Viet Nam. Hardy to 25F.

Pithecellobium flexicaule

Common name	Texas Ebony
Usual height	20'
Spacing	20'
Bloom	Spring; cream
Evergreen	Yes, hardy to 18 - 20F
Exposure	Full sun
Soil	Well draining
Propagation	Seed

Native to south Texas and eastern Mexico, Texas Ebony offers dense, dark-green foliage on light-gray branches. Frothy spring flowers are followed by large dark-brown seed pods.

Although very slow-growing, Texas Ebony eventually develops into an exceptionally attractive tree. Place it where thorny branches won't be a problem. It prefers deep, infrequent waterings.

Pithecellobium mexicanum, Mexican Ebony, resembles an overgrown Catclaw Acacia. Likewise, it has light-gray bark, recurved thorns, gray-green leaves and creamy catkins in the spring.

Its open angular branches will reach 20-30' in height and 20-25' in width. Although fast-growing while young, it tapers off to a moderate growth rate. Watch for scale insects in the summer.

Native to southern Baja California, Sonora and Sinaloa, Mexico. Very drought-tolerant. Hardy to 15-20F.

Pithecellobium pallens, Tenaza, matures quickly to 20-30' high and 15-25' wide. Fragrant, creamy flowers are borne in summer. In winter, it is semi-evergreen.

Tenaza works well in groves, providing light shade. Its upright growth habit and tropical appearance are very different from other Pithecellobium species and it may be hard to find.

Native throughout Mexico and southwest Texas. Hardy to 20F.

Pithecellobium flexicaule

Podranea ricasoliana

Plumbago scandens 'Summer Snow'

Plumbago scandens 'Summer Snow'™

Common name	'Summer Snow' Plumbago
Usual height	3 - 4'
Spacing	3 - 4'
Bloom	Spring and fall; white
Evergreen	No, hardy to 20F
Exposure	Shade
Soil	Any with good drainage
Propagation	Seed / cuttings

'Summer Snow' Plumbago freezes to the ground in winter, but quickly recovers in spring. The contrast of white flowers over the foliage mass has a cooling effect.

Although it performs best in shade, it will tolerate full sun. Place it away from walks as the sticky fruit tends to cling to clothing.

Native to southern Arizona, southern Florida and the tropical Americas at 2,500-4,000'.

Podranea ricasoliana

Common name	Pink-trumpet Vine
Usual height	20'
Spacing	10' minimum
Bloom	Midsummer to frost; pink
Evergreen	No, hardy to 26F
Exposure	Full sun
Soil	Well draining
Propagation	Seed / cuttings

Although it will defoliate or freeze to the ground in winter, Pink-trumpet Vine quickly recovers. Very drought-tolerant once established, it likes the hottest locations. In Tucson, Arizona it can live on rainfall alone.

The summer monsoons bring on large clusters of fragrant pinkish, lavender flowers that stand out against the rich-green foliage. Podranea needs support to climb. Native to South Africa.

Prosopis chilensis

Prosopis alba, Argentine Mesquite, is the most vigorous for landscape use. Young branches bear enormous white spines. Hardy to 18F. Native to Argentina.

P. alba 'Colorado,'™ Colorado Mesquite, is a new introduction that is almost thornless and very fast-growing. Uniformity of trees is ensured through propagation by cuttings. It is reluctantly deciduous, retaining leaves well after all other Mesquite are bare. In warm areas, it may only be partially deciduous.

Due to its upright habit, Colorado Mesquite is easier to maintain than its cousins which grow erratically. Because of these advantages, this selection will probably become the most popular for landscape use.

Prosopis, commonly called *Mesquite*, are some of our hardiest and most useful native trees. (Not all species listed are native.) They adapt to little or abundant water. All have dark-green leaves, rough, dark bark and an interesting form. They produce cream-colored flowers in spring and reach a height of 20-30'. Plant in full sun in any soil at a minimum of 20' apart.

Native Americans make a delicious flour from the dried seed pods, use the wood for cooking, and create strong decoctions from Mesquite plant parts that serve as a disinfectant. Seed pods are also a protein-rich livestock feed.

Colorado is the hardiest of the South American selections, hardy to 14F.

Prosopis velutina

Bees produce tasty honey from Mesquite flowers. The wood is popular for seasoning barbecues.

Prosopis chilensis, Chilean Mesquite, is the species most frequently used in landscaping. True *P. chilensis* resembles a very thorny California Pepper Tree. The trees sold in the nursery industry as Chilean Mesquites are a small-thorned hybrid of several South American species. You may also specify thornless clones. Trunks are twisted. Hardy to 18F.

Prosopis glandulosa* var. *torreyana, Western Honey Mesquite, and *P. glandulosa* var. *glandulosa*, Texas Honey Mesquite, are indiscernable to most people. Each has weeping, twisted branches which give them an exotic appearance similar to California Pepper Tree. Their foliage is brighter green than the other species.

Texas Honey Mesquite has a very long dormant period and is native throughout Texas. Western Honey Mesquite is native to American deserts, primarily the Mojave, and to grasslands up to 5,000'. Both are hardy to 0F.

Prosopis pubescens, Screwbean Mesquite, a shrubby species, is hard to find and slower-growing than others. Its mature bark is very shaggy. The curious twisted, spiral-shape pod is useful in decorations. Flowers are bright yellow.

Native up to 4,000' from West Texas and southern New Mexico to southern California, and into northern Mexico. Hardy to 5-10F.

Prosopis velutina, Arizona or Velvet Mesquite, is the common native Mesquite with gray-green foliage. Nursery stock is limited; salvaged specimens are available, although costly, but the immediate sculptural effect is worth the price. Native at 1,000-4,500' throughout central and southern Arizona. It is slow-growing and hardy to 10F.

Psilostrophe tagetina

Psilostrophe cooperi

Although Psilostrophe cooperi *and* Psilostrophe tagetina *are both commonly referred to as Paper Flower, they are distinguishable by their flower,* P. cooperi *having five petals and* P. tagetina *three.*

Psilostrophe cooperi

Common name	Paper Flower
Usual height	18"
Spacing	2'
Bloom	Spring through fall; yellow
Evergreen	Yes, hardy to 5 - 10F
Exposure	Full sun / light shade
Soil	Any with good drainage
Propagation	Seed / cuttings

Paper Flower responds well to the monsoons. The bright-yellow blossoms eventually dry on the plant and become papery and ivory-colored. Flowers remain attractive for some time after this and give the illusion of a very long bloom period. Peak flowering is in late spring.

Native to the Arizona Upland at 2,000-5,000' and to Utah, western New Mexico, California and northwestern Mexico.

Psilostrophe tagetina, Wooly Paper Flower, is a short-lived perennial. Although more petite than *P. cooperi*, it produces many more flowers. Propagated from seed, it blooms the second year, forming a yellow mound 16" high x 2' wide. Native at 4,000-7,000' in West Texas, eastern Arizona and northern Mexico. Hardy to 0-5F.

Rhus ovata

The red fruit of the Sugar Bush can be used to create a sweet drink. Foliage is pleasantly fragrant.

Rhus ovata

Common name	Sugar Bush
Usual height	12'
Spacing	12'
Bloom	Spring; pink/white
Evergreen	Yes, hardy to 10F
Exposure	Full sun / light shade
Soil	Deep, decomposed granite
Propagation	Seed / cuttings

Very cold- and drought-tolerant, Sugar Bush is native at 3,000-5,000' to central Arizona, southern California and Baja California.

Sugar Bush can be either a large shrub or small tree and makes a good screen. Leaves are deep green and leathery, shaped like a

Rosa banksiae 'Lutea'

Yellow Lady Bank's Rose produces soft-yellow flowers borne in natural nosegay clusters.

partially folded heart. The fragrant foliage is vanilla scented. Sugar Bush is underused in the landscape industry. Plant it in fall or winter to ease establishment. Combine good drainage with judicious summer watering to avoid root rot.

***Rosa banksiae* 'Lutea'**

Common name	Yellow Lady Bank's Rose
Usual height	20'
Spacing	15'+
Bloom	Spring; yellow
Evergreen	Partially, hardy to 10F
Exposure	Full sun / light shade
Soil	Best with minimal rock, caliche.

The world's largest rose bush, "The Tombstone Rose" (Tombstone, Arizona), is a Lady Bank's Rose.

This classic rose, native to China, has endured due to its hardiness. Today it is more popular than ever. A vigorous climber, it quickly covers fences and embankments. The rich-green foliage is nearly evergreen and the branches are thornless. Supplemental watering is essential.

R. banksiae 'Alba plena' is a lightly-fragrant, white-flowered form. Branches have a few thorns. Hardy to 10F.

Neither of these roses require the special care and pruning necessary for most roses.

Rosmarinus officinalis

Bees love Rosemary flowers. The leaves are the portion used for the seasoning.

Ruellia peninsularis

Rosmarinus officinalis

Common name	Rosemary
Usual height	2 - 4'
Spacing	4'
Bloom	Spring and fall; blue, white
Evergreen	Yes, hardy to 7F
Exposure	Full sun / light shade
Soil	Any with drainage
Propagation	Cuttings

Rosemary's stiff upright branches create an interesting form. The narrow, leathery leaves are dark green on top and nearly white beneath. The leaves are the portion used for seasoning. Bees love the flowers. Rabbits won't bother it. Native to the Mediterranean.

R. officinalis prostratus, Dwarf Rosemary, is a low-growing form often used as a groundcover for small areas. It is great trailing over the edge of a raised planter. Mature size is approximately 2 x 5'. With age, it becomes woody and should be replanted. Hardy to 10F.

Several varieties of the species mentioned here are available through herb growers.

Ruellia peninsularis

Common name	Baja Ruellia
Usual height	2 - 4'
Spacing	4'
Bloom	Spring through fall; purple
Evergreen	Yes, in protected areas, hardy to 28F.
Exposure	Full sun / light shade
Soil	Well draining
Propagation	Cuttings

Although its cool-green foliage recovers quickly from frost damage, Ruellia is best when planted in hot, protected areas. Ruellia is drought-tolerant when established.

Blue-purple flowers nearly cover the foliage in spring. Sporadic bloom occurs throughout the warm season. Native to southern Baja California and central Sonora, Mexico.

Salvia chamaedryoides, Mexican Blue Sage, has fine gray foliage on non-woody stems. Mature height is 1-1/2 – 2'. Flower spikes are sky blue. Heaviest bloom is spring and fall. This evergreen is sensitive to over-watering. Native to central Mexico. Hardy to 15F.

Salvia clevelandii, Chaparral Sage, bears deep-blue flowers in tight whorls which are stacked on branch ends like skewered balls. Its fragrant, gray foliage makes a good tea.

Provide minimal supplemental water in summer and prune in the fall. Mature size is 4' x 5'. Native to the coastal arca of southern California and Baja California. Hardy to 19F.

Salvia clevelandii

Salvia coccinea

Salvia coccinea, Cherry-red Sage, freezes to the ground in winter except in very protected areas. Bright-green leaves contrast well with the red flowers which open along branch tips in the morning. By afternoon they are gone. The next morning the cycle is repeated. Mature height is 3'. Hardy to 30F.

S. coccinea is best in a casual garden due to its tendency to reseed. It needs regular watering. Native to the southeastern U.S. and tropical Americas. Hardy to 30F.

Salvia is an interesting genus of attractive, colorful plants. Even *S. officinalis*, the common cooking sage, has beautiful flowers. Hummingbirds love them, but rabbits dislike the pungent foliage.

Some are evergreen and hardiness varies. Those listed here are perennials. Usual height is 1-4'. Red, white or blue flowers appear spring through fall. Plant 2-4' apart in light to full shade with good drainage.

Salvia greggii (both photos)

Because Salvias are non-toxic, the flowers, if organically grown, may be used in salads. Their foliage has a pungent flavor used for seasoning.

Salvia farinacea, Mealy-cup Sage, is dormant in winter, so plant among groundcover for continuous cover or treat as an annual.

Dark-blue flowers form on dense spikes above the green foliage throughout the warm season. A white-flowered form is also available.

Water Mealy-cup Sage regularly. Maximum height is approximately 18". Native to Texas. Hardy to 24-26F.

Salvia greggii, Autumn Sage, is a Chihuahuan Desert native. The fine foliage is dark green. Flower colors available include ruby red, cherry red, and white, among others.

Mature height is approximately 2'. Place it near larger shrubs with gray foliage to highlight flowers and foliage.

As flower spikes bloom out, trim them off for a neater appearance. Prune to shape the plant in early spring.

Autumn Sage prefers light afternoon shade. Be careful not to over-water in summer. Midsummer, fertilize with nitrogen and sulfur to keep it going. *S. greggii* 'Sierra Linda'™ is exceptionally durable. Hardy to 0-5F.

Salvia leucantha (both photos)

Salvia leucantha, Mexican Sage, produces many new branches from the roots each spring. Foliage is gray-green.

In the spring and fall, white flowers encased in fuzzy chenille-like lavender bracts grace the soft branch tips. Stems are nearly white. It dies down in winter in all but the warmest areas.

Mature height is 3-4'. Mexican Sage prefers light shade and needs deep, infrequent irrigation in summer. Once a week is satisfactory in the desert. You can divide crowns. Native to Mexico. Hardy to 24-26F.

Salvia leucophylla, Purple Sage, is similar to *S. clevelandii* but larger to 5' high. Leaves are light gray; flowers are lavender-pink. A hard-to-find species, but worth the search. Don't over-water it in summer. Native to the Coastal Sage Shrub plant community through southern and central California below 2,000'. Hardy to 20F.

***Salvia microphylla* 'Sierra Madre'™** grows into an open shrub 4' high and wide. Its small green leaves are aromatic. White pencil-line, vertical stripes accent the plum-colored stems. Scarlet flowers appear in spring and fall. The selection 'Red Storm'™ only grows to about 3' high.

Calylophus will intertwine with the lower branches when planted near the base.

S. microphylla, a native of the Chihuahuan Desert, is one of the hardiest Salvias. Hardy to 5-10F.

Simmondsia chinensis

Oil from the Jojoba seed is used in cosmetics and lubricants.

Simmondsia chinensis

Common name	Jojoba
Usual height	4 - 6'
Spacing	6'
Bloom	Spring; inconspicuous
Evergreen	Yes, hardy to 18F
Exposure	Full sun
Soil	Any
Propagation	Seed

Jojoba (pronounced ho-HO-bah) is another native to the Sonoran Desert and chaparral at 1,000-5,000' in Arizona, California and Baja California.

Jojoba's dull gray-green leaves are oval-shaped. Seeds — which taste something like filberts — contain an oil which is used in cosmetics and lubricants. The character of the oil is similar to sperm whale oil.

Good as a background shrub, Jojoba can be adapted to an informal screen or formal clipped hedge. It is cold- and drought-tolerant.

Sophora secundiflora

Common name:	Texas Mountain Laurel, Mescal Bean
Usual height	8 - 15'
Spacing	8 - 10'
Bloom	Spring; purple
Evergreen	Yes, hardy to 0-5F
Exposure	Full sun
Soil	Any with good drainage
Propagation	Seed

Glossy, dark-green leaves provide a good year-round screen. Although slow-growing, it can be trained into a small tree.

The large pea-shaped flowers are borne in wisteria-like clusters approximately 8" long. Their fragrance is similar to Juicy Fruit™ gum. Gray-white peanut-shaped seed pods contain bright red seeds which are extremely poisonous. Remove young pods before they mature.

Texas Mountain Laurel is very cold-, drought- and heat-tolerant. Native to the trans-Pecos region of Texas and northern Mexico.

Sophora secundiflora

The fragrance of the beautiful Texas Mountain Laurel flower is similar to Juicy Fruit™ gum.

Desert Mallow is most impressive planted in drifts incorporating a variety of colors. Monet would have appreciated the effect.

Sphaeralcea ambigua

Sphaeralcea ambigua

Sphaeralcea ambigua

Common name	Desert or Globe Mallow
Usual height	3'
Spacing	3'+
Bloom:	Spring; pink, orange, rose, white, lavender, coral, red
Evergreen	Yes, hardy to 4 to 5F
Exposure	Full sun / light shade
Soil	Any
Propagation	Seed / cuttings

Widely distributed throughout the Southwest below 3,500', Globe Mallow is one of the earliest spring flowers. The orange-flowered clone is most frequently found as a "weed" in neglected southwest urban areas. Various other colors are native around Florence Junction and Picacho Peak in south-central Arizona and other locations.

The blue-green leaves are supported by upright branches with flowers at the end. They may be annual or perennial depending on water availability.

Allow Desert Mallow to reseed so that new plants with surprising flower colors can replace declining ones. For neatness, plants may be pruned nearly to the ground following flowering. They will quickly regrow attractive foliage.

Some supplemental water is necessary to maintain foliage.

Stachys coccinea

The exceptionally long bloom season of Texas Betony delights both humans and hummingbirds.

Without water, the foliage will dry up. New shoots will appear with the rain.

Stachys coccinea

Common name	Scarlet or Texas Betony
Usual height	1'
Spacing	2 - 3'
Bloom	Spring through fall; coral-red
Evergreen	Yes, hardy to 10F
Exposure	Light to medium shade
Soil	Damp
Propagation	Cuttings / seed

Native to riparian springs and seeps at 1,500-8,000' in southwest Texas, New Mexico and Arizona. Texas Betony adapts well to moist, shady landscape areas. Soft, sage-green stems and leaves form small mounds. Colorful flowers are held above the foliage on 4-6" spikes. Remove spent flower spikes.

Use Texas Betony selectively in shady, protected areas near outdoor living areas.

Tagetes palmeri with *Salvia greggii* at right.

This perennial marigold is native to various mountain ranges of the Sonoran and Chihuahuan Deserts.

Tagetes lucida, Mexican Tarragon/Mt. Atlas Anise, doesn't look like a marigold. Rich-green leaves are long and narrow on stiff and vertical branches that form a very compact plant. In fall bright-yellow, compact, daisy-like flowers color the branch ends. It is slower to recover from frost than *T. palmeri*.

The Tarahumara Indians of western Chihuahua, Mexico dry the leaves for a delicious tea. A 3" sprig of fresh foliage will also flavor sun tea. For a strong anise flavor, substitute *T. lucida* leaves for tarragon in recipes.

Native to the western Sierra Madre of Mexico. Hardy to 32F.

Tagetes palmeri (lemmoni)

Common name	Mountain Marigold
Usual height	3 - 5'
Spacing	4 - 5'
Bloom	Fall; yellow
Evergreen	No, hardy to 30F
Exposure	Full sun
Soil	Any
Propagation	Seed / cuttings

This perennial marigold is native to southeastern Arizona. When frozen to the ground, it quickly recovers with warm weather. The lacy foliage is dark green and fragrant with the typical marigold scent.

In fall, the entire plant is encased with brilliant-yellow, daisy-like flowers which, although good for cutting, may irritate allergy sufferers.

Use to enhance the mini-oasis effect. To prevent splayed branches, watch watering and cut back to control growth.

Tecoma stans* var. *angustata, commonly called Yellow-trumpet Bush or Esperanza, is the narrow-leafed form. Flowers are smaller than *T. stans* var. *stans* and persist throughout the warm season. Seed pods usually don't develop until late summer.

Mature height is about 6-8'. Native at 3,000-5,000 from southern Arizona to the trans-Pecos region of Texas. Hardy to 30F.

Tecoma stans var. *angustata*

***Tecoma stans* var. *stans*,** Yellow Bells, is a large sprawling shrub 10-20' in height that needs lots of room. With a little work, it can be espaliered. Although the lush green foliage can be damaged by frost, recovery is quick. Large clusters of bright-yellow trumpet flowers provide color through spring and fall.

Plant in full sun 10' or more apart in deep soil. To encourage flowering, fertilize regularly and cut off spent flower clusters to prevent seed development. Seed pods are unsightly in winter.

Yellow Bells can be propagated by seed or cuttings. Native to tropical America. Hardy to 28F.

Trichocereus huascha hybrid

Trichocereus candicans

Trichocereus are the best-kept secret of cactophiles.

Trichocereus candicans

Common name	Trichocereus
Usual height	2'
Spacing	4'+
Bloom	Spring to summer, white
Evergreen	Yes, hardy to 10F
Exposure	Light shade
Soil	Any with drainage
Propagation	Seed / cuttings

Trichocereus look like overgrown hedgehog cactus. Rich-green skin is protected by short spines. New shoots sprout from the base eventually forming a broad mass.

Large 6-8" flowers open in the evening and remain open to midmorning. Water weekly and fertilize monthly during the warm season to encourage bloom. Native to northern Argentina.

***Trichocereus huascha* hybrid** is similar in form. Flowers are a fusion of scarlet, fuchsia and red-orange.

Many other hybrids in exotic colors are available though hard to find. Look for them at botanical garden sales. Hardy to 19F.

Ulmus parvifolia

Ulmus parvifolia

Common name	Evergreen or Chinese Elm
Usual height	40'
Spacing	40'
Bloom	Insignificant
Evergreen	Semi, hardy to 10 - 25F
Exposure	Full sun
Soil	Deep soil with good drainage
Propagation	Cuttings

This is an excellent canopy tree having long, arching branches with weeping ends that move with the breeze. The dark-green foliage is partly deciduous. Keep the top thinned out to prevent wind damage. Its attractive bark is mottled gray and terra cotta. Evergreen Elm's graceful form makes it attractive as a patio or street tree.

Ungnadia speciosa

Use Mexican Buckeye as a garden focal point or small patio tree. Look for this hardy, very slow-growing gem at botanical garden plant sales.

Vauquelinia californica

Ungnadia speciosa

Common name	Mexican Buckeye
Usual height	15'
Spacing	15'
Bloom	Spring; purple
Evergreen	No, hardy to 5 - 10F
Exposure	Full sun
Soil	Any
Propagation	Seed

This native of Texas, New Mexico and northern Mexico grows into a large shrub or small tree. The light-gray bark contrasts with the long, dark-green, deeply-cut leaves. In spring, clusters of small, pea-shaped purple flowers are quite showy resembling Redbud from a distance.

The fruit is a woody three-lobed pod which can be dried and used for decoration, although its seeds are poisonous.

Vauquelinia californica

Common name	Arizona Rosewood
Usual height	10 - 2 0'
Spacing	10'+
Bloom	Spring; white
Evergreen	Yes, hardy to 5 - 10F
Exposure	Full sun, light shade
Soil	Any
Propagation	Seed / cuttings

The extremely cold- and drought-tolerant Arizona Rosewood slowly grows into a large, dense screen. Leathery, dark-green leaves are long and narrow. Tiny flowers form in clusters.

Arizona Rosewood is good as a hardy transition shrub. Native at 2,500-5,000' in central Arizona and northern Mexico.

Verbena rigida

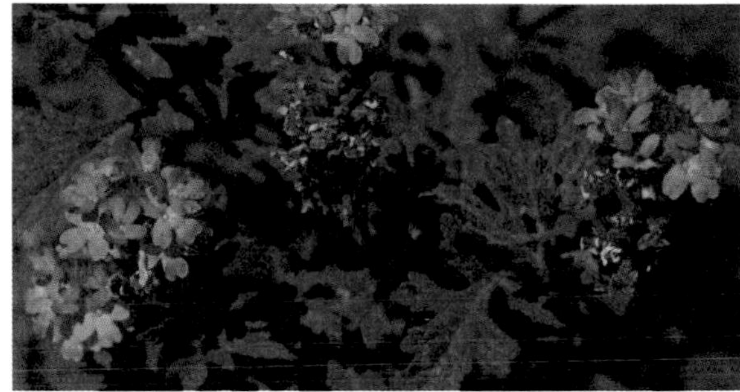

Verbena gooddingii

Verbena tenera

Verbena gooddingii (Glandularia gooddingii), Goodding Verbena, is native to a large portion of the Southwest between 3,000' and 5,000'. Fragrant pale-lavender blooms occur spring through fall. Foliage is medium green. Drought will kill this species quickly, but it is hardy to 5F.

Verbena peruviana, Peruvian Verbena, is a perennial groundcover forming a very flat dark-green mat. Although available in many colors, 'Sissinghurst' and other varieties with bright-pink flowers seem to do best in the desert. Native to South America including Peru, Uruguay and southern Brazil. Hardy to 24F.

Verbena rigida, Sandpaper Verbena, has coarse leaves and stiff upright branches. It is the hardiest and most vigorous of the genus due to growth on stolons. It is very long-lived. The foliage mass may become 3' high. To control it, cut back severely cut back severely after each flush of bloom. To neaten the appearance, cut to the ground in early spring. *V. rigida* is good for erosion control. Flowers are a vivid purple. Native to Argentina. Hardy to 15F.

Verbena is found at many altitudes. Plants range in size and vigor depending on available water. Because they are herbaceous, not woody, they generally have a life of 2-3 years. Plan on occasional replacement in the landscape. Usual height is 1-2'. Pink or purple flowers bloom spring to fall. Verbena are evergreen. Plant 3-4' apart in full sun or light shade in any soil except caliche. Verbena can be propagated by seed or cuttings.

V. gooddingii, *V. rigida* and *V. tenera* will reseed and naturalize. Provide regular irrigation for best appearance. Trim back spent flower stems and fertilize to encourage rebloom. You can collect and dry flowering branches to make a tea which is good seasoned with mint and honey.

Verbena tenera (V. pulchella var. gracilior), Rock Verbena, has finely cut, dark-green foliage. Flowers may be purple, pink or white. It reseeds freely. Rock Verbena is particularly beautiful when interplanted with *Zinnia grandiflora*. Native to South America. Hardy to 20F.

Skeleton-leaf Goldeneye is tolerant of reflected heat and alkaline soils. Although lush in appearance, it is very drought-tolerant.

Viguiera stenoloba

Viguiera stenoloba

Common name	Skeleton-leaf Goldeneye
Usual height	3 - 4'
Spacing	4'
Bloom	Summer through fall; yellow
Evergreen	Usually, hardy to 5 - 10F
Exposure	Full sun
Soil	Any
Propagation	Seed / cuttings

Of the several Viguiera species native to the southwestern U.S., this is the showiest. Its effect is similar to yellow margarite. The large, bright-yellow, daisy-like flowers persist from late spring until frost.

Selective pruning will keep it within bounds and dense. Skeleton-leaf Goldeneye combines nicely with *Salvia greggii* and *Verbena rigida*.

Native to the trans-Pecos region of Texas and northern Mexico.

Vitex agnus-castus

Vitex agnus-castus

Common name	Chaste Tree, Monk's Pepper
Usual height	10 - 20'
Spacing	20'
Bloom	Spring - summer; pink, lavender, white,
Evergreen	No, hardy to 5 - 10F
Exposure	Full sun
Soil	Any
Propagation	Seed / cuttings

Vitex is usually multi-trunked, eventually forming a small tree. Bark is light gray. Leaves are medium-green above and gray beneath. The palmate-leaf form provides interesting texture. Flower spikes are showy. The foliage is fragrant although it is offensive to some. Seeds resemble peppercorns.

Chaste Tree reseeds freely where moisture is available. Don't plant near walks or patios as droppage is year around. Round seeds are hazardous on sidewalks. Native to southern Europe.

Vitex triangularis, Sonoran Vitex, forms a large shrub. Its roundish leaves are medium-green above and gray beneath. Leaves feel nice to touch. Small clusters of purple flowers persist from summer to frost. It suffers damage when temperatures drop below 25F.

Washingtonia robusta is the most widely planted palm in the Southwest.

Washingtonia robusta

Washingtonia robusta

Common name	Mexican Fan Palm
Usual height	40 - 100'
Spacing	20'+
Bloom	Summer
Evergreen	Yes, hardy to 20F
Exposure	Full sun
Soil	Any
Propagation	Seed

The rich-green fronds of the Mexican Fan Palm are fan-shaped. The tree is fast growing and hardy to 20F. It's effective as a street tree when alternated with a canopy tree and especially beautiful in clusters of three to five plants. Mature height is 100'.

If young plants are tilted, new growth will be upright, creating a curved trunk. Flower stalks are a nuisance, producing small black seeds which sprout everywhere. Cut them off while they're young. *W. robusta* is native to central Baja California.

W. filifera, California Fan Palm, is native to remote canyons and oases along the Arizona-California border and northern Baja California. Its trunk is

Yucca rigida

considerably more robust than the Mexican Fan Palm. Mature height is 60'.

California Fan Palms are best when planted simply to line streets or drives. Outside of historic urban areas, they are hard to find. Hardy to 18F.

Whether a small accent shrub or a tree, all *Yucca* have distinctive texture. Leaves are long, narrow and leathery and may be stiff or pliable. Yucca blend with either desert or tropical landscapes. Usual height can be 4-20'. White blooms occur in spring. Plant in full sun in any soil with good drainage. Yucca can be propagated by seed, offset or cuttings. They are evergreen.

Yucca aloifolia, Spanish Bayonet, becomes a large sprawling plant to 10' high x 10' wide. Stiff, dense leaves are medium green with sharp points. Give it lots of room away from walkways. Quite dramatic at night when backlit. Variegated form has cream and white streaks along leaves. Cut back to control size. Y. *aloifolia* blooms only when drought-stressed. Native to the southeastern U.S., the Carribean and Mexico. Hardy to 9-18F.

Yucca elata

Yucca baccata, Banana Yucca, is named for its edible banana-shaped fruit. It is native to elevations between 3,000' and 8,000' throughout the Southwest. Native Americans used the leaf fibers to make cordage.

Mature height is approximately 4'. Clumps may become over 15' wide with age. Tall white flower spikes occur in March to April. Hardy to 5-10F.

Yucca brevifolia, Joshua Tree, grows slowly to about 20'. Stiff, gray-green leaves clothe angular branches. Old leaves point down the branches. Short flower spikes appear in February to March.

Plant Y. *brevifolia* in a dry, well-drained area.

Joshua Tree is native up to 3,500' in the Mojave Desert. Usually only salvaged specimens are available. Because this species is protected, be sure the appropriate state tags are on any plants you purchase. Don't buy if tags are not available; report the seller to the Department of Agriculture.

Occasionally nursery-grown stock is available in one- and five-gallon containers. These do not require tags. Hardy to 0F.

Yucca elata, Soap-tree Yucca, is native at 1,500-6,000' to central and southeastern Arizona, across southern New Mexico and southwest Texas. Slow-growing to 20', the trunk may be single or with a few branches.

Blue-green leaves may be up to 4' long and 1/2" wide. Together they form hemispheres at the ends of the branches. Old leaves droop down along sides of the branches. April bloom is on very tall spikes.

Small, nursery-grown or large salvaged plants are available. State tags are required on salvaged plants. Hardy to -5F.

Yucca recurvifolia, Pendulous Yucca, is readily available. Its soft form works with either desert or tropical landscapes. This Yucca tolerates both sun and shade and may rebloom in the fall. Native to the south-eastern U.S.. Hardy to 5-9F.

Yucca rigida, Blue Yucca, has stiff blue-gray leaves with sharp points. It grows slowly to a width of about 3' and height of 12'. Blue Yucca is extremely cold- and drought-tolerant. Native to the Chihuahuan Desert, it is hardy to 10F.

Yucca rostrata, Beard Yucca, is also a Chihuahuan Desert native. Its foliage is thinner and more flexible than Y. *rigida*. Yellow margins border the attractive blue-green foliage. Hardy to 5F.

Zauschneria californica subspecies *latifolia*

Common name	California Fuchsia, Hummingbird Trumpet
Usual height	1 - 2'
Spacing	3'
Bloom	Summer through fall; brilliant orange
Evergreen	No, hardy to 32F
Exposure	Full sun / light shade
Soil	Any with moisture
Propagation	Seed / cuttings

Look for this Arizona and California native in riparian areas with year-round water. Plants may be scraggly or lush depending on water availability. Foliage is sage green. Tubular, fluorescent-orange flowers persist until frost. Native generally at 2,500-7,000'.

It is best to cut back the entire plant to the ground for winter. With age, the clump gets wider. Hummingbirds love it.

Zauschneria californica ssp. *latifolia*

Zinnia grandiflora

Common name	Prairie Zinnia
Usual height	Less than 1'
Spacing	3'
Bloom	Warm season; yellow orange
Evergreen	Yes, hardy to 10F
Exposure	Full sun
Soil	Any
Propagation	Seed / cuttings

Native to natural grasslands at 4,000-6,000' throughout the Midwest and Southwest United States, Prairie Zinnia would be indistinguishable were it not for the zingy yellow flowers produced in profusion through the warm season.

The narrow soft-green leaves blend with surrounding plants. It forms small mounds and spreads by stolons. A great effect can be created by interplanting Z. *grandiflora* with Verbena.

Zinnia grandiflora

How to Use Plant Tables

The tables on pages 101 through 120, known as *matrices* to professionals, provide an overview of many of the plants included in this book.

Plants are separated into five growth categories: trees, shrubs, groundcovers, accents and vines.

Information about size, appearance, life factors, potential problems and appropriate landscape zone is provided. Use the tables for preliminary selection of several possible choices.

Then turn back to the plant descriptions for photos and more detailed information as you make your final decision on what to plant.

A few categories need further explanation.

Hardiness—This is the temperature at which a plant *may* start to suffer frost damage. External factors such as recent daytime temperature, drought and length of time cold temperature is mainatined can affect hardiness year to year.

An entry such as "<18" means the plant is typically hardy to temperatures lower than 18F.

Mini-oasis landscape zone—Put the highest-water-use-landscape zone adjacent to your outdoor living area for greatest appreciation and cooling effect.

Transition landscape zone—Plant selection blends lush green appearance of mini-oasis with drier arid-zone plants.

Arid landscape zone—Composed of native and introduced plants which theoretically can survive on rainfall once established.

Lawn—Located adjacent to mini-oasis for ease of maintenance. Only trees should be planted in grass. Note that many trees do not thrive in turf.

Revegetation—This is the restoration of disturbed areas to their natural condition. It is essential that plant selection is native to the specific site.

Transition from landscaped area to natural desert is helped by use of native plants within the fenced area. A nice contrast of color and texture is visually interesting. Both sunny and shady seating areas are provided. This landscape in Scottsdale, Arizona was designed by Mary Hoffman.

Trees

Mother Nature's sculpture — *Acacia greggii*. This tree in Paradise Valley, Arizona is recognized in the American Forests National Register of Big Trees as a National Champion. The tree was nominated by the author.

Trees

	SIZE	APPEARANCE				LIFE FACTORS				PROBLEMS			LANDSCAPE ZONES				
Botanical Name **Common Name**	Height x Width (feet)	Flower Season	Flower Color	Foliage Texture	Foliage Color	Hardiness (degrees F)	Growth Rate	Water Use	Evergreen	Litter	Thorns	Allergenic	Mini-oasis	Transition	Arid	Lawn	Revegetation
Acacia abyssinica Abyssinian Acacia	25x25	Spr	White	Fine	Green	18-20	Slow	Mod		Min			•	•			
Acacia aneura Mulga	20x12	Spr-Fall	Yellow	Med	Gray	10	Slow	Low	•	Min				•	•		
Acacia berlandieri Guajillo, Berlandier Acacia	15x15	Spr	White	Fine	Green	15-20	Mod	Low		Mod	Few		•	•	•		
Acacia salicina Cooba, Weeping Wattle	25x15	Fall	White	Med	Green	18	Fast	Low	•	Min			•	•			
Acacia smallii (*A. minuta*) Desert Sweet Acacia	20x20	Win	Yellow	Fine	Dark green	12	Mod	Low	•	High	•		•	•	•		•
Acacia stenophylla Shoestring Acacia	30x20	Fall	White	Med	Blue-green	18	Fast	L-M	•	Min			•	•	•	•	
Acacia willardiana Palo Blanco	20x10	Spr	White	Fine	Green	25	Mod	L-M	•	Min			•	•			
Brahea armata Mexican Blue Palm	40x16	Spr	White	Coarse	Blue	18	Slow	L-M	•	Min			•	•		•	
Brahea edulis Guadalupe Palm	30x16	Spr	White	Coarse	Green	<20	Slow	L-M	•	Min			•	•		•	
Caesalpinia cacalaco Cascalote	15x15	Win	Yellow	Med	Green	25	Slow	L-M	•	Min	•			•			
Cercidium floridum Blue Palo Verde	30x30	Spr	Yellow	Fine	Blue-green	10	Fast	L-M		Mod	•		•	•	•		•
Cercidium microphyllum Little-leaf Palo Verde, Foothill Palo Verde	20x20	Spr	Yellow	Fine	Yellow-green	12-15	Slow	Low		Mod	•			•	•		•
Cercidium praecox Palo Brea, Sonoran Palo Verde	20x30	Spr	Yellow	Fine	Lime-green	20	Mod	Low	Semi	Min	•		•	•	•		
Chilopsis linearis Desert Willow	25x20	Spr-Fall	Lavender	Med	Green	0	Fast	Mod		Mod			•		•		•
Chorisia speciosa Silk-floss Tree	60x30	Fall	Pink	Coarse	Green	26-28	Mod	Mod		Min	•		•			•	
Eucalyptus erythrocorys Red-cap Gum, Illarie	30x20	Sum	Yellow	Med	Green	28	Mod	L-M	•	Min			•	•			

Trees

Botanical Name Common Name	SIZE	APPEARANCE				LIFE FACTORS				PROBLEMS			LANDSCAPE ZONES				
	Height x Width (feet)	Flower Season	Flower Color	Foliage Texture	Foliage Color	Hardiness (degrees F)	Growth Rate	Water Use	Evergreen	Litter	Thorns	Allergenic	Mini-oasis	Transition	Arid	Lawn	Revegetation
Eucalyptus formanii Forman's Eucalyptus	15x15	Spr	White	Fine	Gray-green	15	Slow	Low	•	Min				•			
Eucalyptus leucoxylon 'Rosea' White Ironbark	30x20	Fall	Red	Med	Blue-green	14-18	Mod	Low	•	Min				•			
Eucalyptus spathulata Narrow-leaf Gimlet	20x20	Spr	White	Fine	Olive	18-26	Mod	Low	•	Min			•	•			
Eucalyptus torquata Coral Gum	20x20	Spr	Coral	Med	Blue-green	17-21	Mod	Low	•	Min			•	•			
Eucalyptus woodwardii Woodward's Black Butt, Lemon-flowered Gum	40x15	Fall-Spr	Yellow	Coarse	Gray	17-22	Mod	Low	•	Min			•	•			
Leucaena retusa Golden Ball Lead Tree	20x20	Spr	Yellow gold	Med	Green	10	Mod	L-M	Semi	Min			•	•			
Lysiloma microphylla v. thornberi Desert Fern, Feather Bush	15x12	Spr	White	Fine	Green	22-24	Mod	L-M		Min			•	•			
Olneya tesota Desert Ironwood	30x30	Spr	Lavender	Fine	Gray-green	20-22	Slow	Low		Min	•			•	•		•
Opuntia ficus-indica Indian Fig	10x10	Spr	Yellow	Coarse	Green	20	Mod	Low	•	Min	•			•	•		
Phoenix dactylifera Date Palm	40x20	Sum	N/A	Coarse	Gray-green	15	Mod	L-M	•	Mod	•		•	•	•	•	
Phoenix roebelenii Pigmy Date Palm	8x4	N/A	N/A	Fine	Green	25	Slow	Mod	•	Min			•				
Pithecellobium flexicaule Texas Ebony	20x20	Spr	Cream	Fine	Dark green	18-20	Slow	L-M	•	Min	•		•	•	•		
Pithecellobium mexicanum Mexican Ebony	30x25	Spr	Cream	Fine	Gray-green	15-20	Fast-Mod	L-M	Semi	Min-Mod			•	•	•		
Pithecellobium pallens Tenaza	30x25	Sum	Cream	Fine	Gray-green	20	Fast	L-M	Semi	Mod	•		•	•	•		
Prosopis alba Argentine Mesquite	30x30	Spr	Cream	Fine	Dark green	18	Fast	L-M		Mod	•	•	•	•	•	•	•

Trees

	SIZE	APPEARANCE				LIFE FACTORS				PROBLEMS			LANDSCAPE ZONES				
Botanical Name Common Name	Height x Width (feet)	Flower Season	Flower Color	Foliage Texture	Foliage Color	Hardiness (degrees F)	Growth Rate	Water Use	Evergreen	Litter	Thorns	Allergenic	Mini-oasis	Transition	Arid	Lawn	Revegetation
Prosopis alba 'Colorado'™ Colorado Mesquite	30x30	Spr	Cream	Fine	Dark green	14	Fast	L-M	•	Mod		•	•	•	•	•	•
Prosopis chilensis Chilean Mesquite	30x30	Spr	Cream	Fine	Dark green	18	Fast	L-M		Mod	•	•	•	•	•	•	•
Prosopis glandulosa v. glandulosa Texas Honey Mesquite	20x20	Spr	Cream	Fine	Green	0	Fast	L-M		Mod	•	•	•	•	•	•	
Prosopis glandulosa v. torreyana Western Honey Mesquite	20x20	Spr	Cream	Fine	Green	0	Fast	L-M		Mod	•	•	•	•	•	•	
Prosopis pubescens Screwbean Mesquite	20x20	Spr	Yellow	Fine	Green	5-10	Mod	L-M		Mod	•	•	•	•	•		•
Prosopis velutina Arizona Mesquite, Velvet Mesquite	30x30	Spr	Cream	Fine	Green	10	Slow	L-M		Mod	•	•	•	•	•	•	•
Rhus ovata Sugar Bush	12x12	Spr	Pink	Med	Green	10	Slow	L-M	•	Min				•	•		
Sophora secundiflora Texas Mt. Laurel Mescal Bean	15x10	Spr	Purple	Med	Green	0-5	Slow	L-M	•	Min			•	•	•		
Ulmus parvifolia Chinese Elm, Evergreen Elm	40x40	N/A	N/A	Fine	Dark green	10-25	Fast	Mod	Semi	Mod			•	•		•	
Ungnadia speciosa Mexican Buckeye	15x15	Spr	Red-violet	Coarse	Dark green	5-10	Slow	L-M		Min			•	•			
Vitex agnus-castus Chaste Tree, Monk's Pepper	20x20	Spr	White, Pink, Purple	Med	Dark green	5-10	Mod	L-M		High			•	•	•	•	
Washingtonia filifera California Fan Palm	60x15	Spr	N/A	Coarse	Green	18	Fast	L-M	•	Mod	•		•	•		•	
Washingtonia robusta Mexican Fan Palm	100x15	Spr	N/A	Coarse	Green	20	Fast	L-M	•	Mod	•		•	•		•	
Yucca brevifolia Joshua Tree	30x15	Spr	White	Med	Blue-green	0	Slow	Low	•	Min	•				•		
Yucca elata Soap-tree Yucca	20x10	Spr	White	Med	Blue-green	-5to0	Slow	Low	•	Min	•			•	•		•

Shrubs

Colorful combination of *Salvia leucantha*, *Zauschneria californica* and *Verbena rigida*.

Shrubs

	SIZE	APPEARANCE				LIFE FACTORS				PROBLEMS			LANDSCAPE ZONES				
Botanical Name Common Name	Height x Width (feet)	Flower Season	Flower Color	Foliage Texture	Foliage Color	Hardiness (degrees F)	Growth Rate	Water Use	Evergreen	Litter	Thorns	Allergenic	Mini-oasis	Transition	Arid	Lawn	Revegetation
Acacia rigens Needle Acacia	6x6	Spr	Yellow	Fine	Gray-green	20	Mod	L-M	•	Min				•	•		
Anisacanthus quadrifidus v. breviloibus 'Mountain Flame'™	5x5	Sum-Fall	Red	Med	Green	<10	Mod	Mod		Min			•	•			
Anisacanthus quadrifidus v. wrightii 'Mexican Flame'™	5x5	Sum-Fall	Red-orange	Med	Green	<20	Mod	Mod		Min			•	•			
Bougainvillea brasiliensis Bougainvillea	6x20	Spr-Fall	Varies	Med	Green	32	Fast	L-M		Mod	•		•	•	•		
Caesalpinia gilliesii Desert Bird of Paradise	5x5	Sum-Fall	Yellow	Fine	Green	5-10	Slow	Low		Min			•	•	•		
Caesalpinia mexicana Mexican Bird of Paradise	10x6	Spr-Fall	Yellow	Fine	Dark green	18	Fast	L-M	•	Mod			•	•	•		
Caesalpinia pulcherrima Red Bird of Paradise	6x6	Sum-Fall	Orange	Fine	Dark green	30	Fast	L-M		Mod			•	•	•		
Calliandra californica (C. peninsularis) Baja-red Fairy Duster	5x5	Spr-Win	Red	Fine	Dark green	26	Mod	L-M	Semi	Min			•	•	•		
Calliandra eriophylla Fairy Duster	3x4	Spr & Fall	White, Pink	Fine	Dark green	0-10	Mod	L-M		Min				•	•		•
Cassia artemisioides Feathery Cassia	6x6	Spr	Yellow	Fine	Gray	15-20	Fast	L-M	•	Mod				•	•		
Cassia biflora (Senna pallida) Twin-flower Cassia, Sonoran Cassia	6x6	Spr-Fall	Yellow	Fine	Dark green	25	Mod	L-M		Mod					•		
Cassia candolleana New Zealand Cassia	6x6	Fall	Yellow	Med	Dark green	20	Mod	L-M	•	Mod			•	•	•		
Cassia goldmanii (Senna polyantha) Goldman's Cassia	6x4	Sum	Yellow	Fine	Bronze-green	20	Mod	L-M		Mod				•	•		
Cassia nemophila Desert Cassia	6x6	Spr	Yellow	Fine	Gray-green	19	Fast	L-M	•	Mod				•	•		
Cassia phyllodenia Silver-leaf Cassia	6x6	Spr	Yellow	Med	Silver	22	Fast	L-M	•	Mod				•	•		

Shrubs

	SIZE	APPEARANCE				LIFE FACTORS				PROBLEMS			LANDSCAPE ZONES				
Botanical Name **Common Name**	Height x Width (feet)	Flower Season	Flower Color	Foliage Texture	Foliage Color	Hardiness (degrees F)	Growth Rate	Water Use	Evergreen	Litter	Thorns	Allergenic	Mini-oasis	Transition	Arid	Lawn	Revegetation
Cassia wislizenii (Senna wislizenii) Shrubby Cassia	10x6	Spr-Fall	Yellow	Fine	Dark green	0-5	Mod	L-M		Mod				•	•		•
Cordia boissieri Anacahuita	10x10	Spr-Fall	White	Coarse	Dark blue-grn	22	Mod	L-M	•	Mod			•	•			
Cordia parvifolia Little-leaf Cordia	5x8	Spr-Fall	White	Med	Dark blue-grn	18	Mod	L-M		Min				•	•		
Dalea frutescens 'Sierra Negra'™ Black Dalea	3x5	Fall	Rose-purple	Fine	Silver-green	0	Mod	Min		Min				•	•		
Dalea greggii Trailing Indigo	1x6	Spr	Purple	Fine	Gray	0-5	Fast	L	•	Min				•	•		
Dalea pulchra Pea Bush	4x5	Win-Spr	Purple	Fine	Gray	10	Mod	L-M	•	Min			•	•	•		•
Dalea versicolor v. sessilis	5x5	Spr-Fall	Purple	Fine	Green	5	Mod	Min	•	Min			•	•	•		
Dodonaea viscosa Hop Bush	12x10	Spr	N/A	Med	Green	10	Mod	L-M	•	Min				•	•		•
Dodonaea viscosa purpurea Purple Hop Bush	12x6	Spr	N/A	Med	Purple	20	Mod	L-M	•	Min				•	•		
Encelia farinosa Brittlebush	3x4	Spr	Yellow	Coarse	Silver	26	Fast	L-M		Min				•	•		•
Eremophila decipiens Poverty Bush	2x3	Spr	Red	Fine	Green	<19	Mod	L-M	•	Min			•	•			
Eremophila glabra 'Murchison River' Poverty Bush	2x3	Spr	Orange	Med	Gray	<21	Mod	L-M	•	Min			•	•			
Ericameria (Haplopappus) laricifolia Turpentine Bush	2x2	Fall	Yellow	Fine	Yellow-green	15-20	Mod	L-M	•	Min				•	•		•
Fouquieria splendens Ocotillo	20x15	Spr	Red-orange	Fine	Green	0-5	Slow	L-M		Min	•				•		•
Justicia californica Chuparosa	6x6	Spr & Fall	Red-orange	Med	Sage-green	28	Mod	L-M	•	Min				•	•		•
Justicia spicigera Mexican Honeysuckle	3x4	Spr-Fall	Orange	Med	Sage-green	19	Mod	L-M	•	Min			•	•	•		

Shrubs

Botanical Name / Common Name	SIZE	APPEARANCE				LIFE FACTORS				PROBLEMS			LANDSCAPE ZONES				
	Height x Width (feet)	Flower Season	Flower Color	Foliage Texture	Foliage Color	Hardiness (degrees F)	Growth Rate	Water Use	Evergreen	Litter	Thorns	Allergenic	Mini-oasis	Transition	Arid	Lawn	Revegetation
Lantana camara Lantana	5x5	Spr-Fall	Varies	Med	Green	30	Fast	L-M		Min			•	•	•		
Larrea divaricata (L. tridentata) Creosote Bush	8x6	Spr-Fall	Yellow	Fine	Olive	0-5	Slow	Low	•	Min				•	•		•
Leucophyllum candidum 'Silver Cloud'™ Silver Cloud Sage	5x5	Sum-Fall	Purple	Fine	Silver	10-15	Mod	L-M	•	Min			•	•	•		
Leucophyllum candidum 'Thunder Cloud'™ Thunder Cloud Sage	3x3	Sum-Fall	Dark Purple	Med	Silver	5-10	Mod	L-M	•	Min			•	•	•		
Leucophyllum frutescens Texas Sage, Cenizo	6x6	Spr-Fall	Lav-pink	Fine	Gray	5-10	Mod	L-M	•	Min			•	•	•		
Leucophyllum frutescens compacta Compact Texas Sage	5x5	Spr-Fall	Lav-pink	Fine	Gray	5-10	Mod	L-M	•	Min			•	•	•		
Leucophyllum frutescens 'Green Cloud'™ Green Cloud Sage	6x6	Spr-Fall	Red-violet	Fine	Sage-green	5-10	Fast	L-M	•	Min			•	•	•		
Leucophyllum frutescens 'White Cloud'™ White Cloud Sage	6x6	Spr-Fall	White	Fine	Gray	5-10	Fast	L-M	•	Min			•	•	•		
Leucophyllum hybrid 'Rain Cloud'™ Rain Cloud Sage	6x4	Spr-Fall	Blue-violet	Med	Gray	5-10	Mod	L-M	•	Min				•	•		
Leucophyllum laevigatum Chihuahuan Sage	6x6	Spr-Fall	Laven-der	Fine	Dark green	10-15	Fast	L-M	•	Min				•	•		
Leucophyllum lang-maniae 'Rio Bravo'™ Rio Bravo Sage	5x5	Sum-Fall	Violet	Fine	Green	5-10	Mod	L-M	•	Min				•	•		
Leucophyllum pruinosum 'Sierra Bouquet'™ Sierra Bouquet Sage	6x6	Sum-Fall	Blue	Fine	Gray	5-10	Mod	L-M	•	Min				•			
Leucophyllum zygo-phyllum 'Blue Ranger' Blue Ranger	3x3	Spr-Fall	Blue-violet	Fine	Dark green	5-10	Mod	L-M	•	Min				•	•		

Shrubs

Botanical Name / Common Name	SIZE	APPEARANCE				LIFE FACTORS				PROBLEMS			LANDSCAPE ZONES				
	Height x Width (feet)	Flower Season	Flower Color	Foliage Texture	Foliage Color	Hardiness (degrees F)	Growth Rate	Water Use	Evergreen	Litter	Thorns	Allergenic	Mini-oasis	Transition	Arid	Lawn	Revegetation
Lysiloma microphyllum v. thornberi Desert Fern, Feather Bush	15x12	Spr	White	Fine	Green	22-24	Mod	L-M		Min			•	•	•		
Nandina domestica Heavenly Bamboo	6x4	Spr	White	Med	Bronze-green	5-10	Slow	Mod	•	Min			•				
Nandina domestica 'compacta'	4x3	Spr	White	Med	Bronze-green	5-10	Slow	Mod	•	Min			•				
Nerium oleander Oleander	15x15	Spr-Fall	Varies	Coarse	Dark green	20	Fast	L-M	•	Mod		•	•	•	•		
Nerium oleander 'Little Red'	6x8	Spr-Fall	Dark Red	Med	Dark green	20	Fast	L-M	•	Mod		•	•	•	•		
Nerium oleander 'Mrs.Roeding'	8x10	Spr-Fall	Coral	Med	Dark green	20	Fast	L-M	•	Mod		•	•	•	•		
Nerium oleander 'Petite Pink'	6x6	Spr-Fall	Pink	Med	Dark green	26	Fast	L-M	•	Mod		•	•	•	•		
Nerium oleander 'Petite Salmon'	6x6	Spr-Fall	Salmon	Med	Dark green	26	Fast	L-M	•	Mod		•	•	•	•		
Plumbago scandens 'Summer Snow'™ Summer Snow Plumbago	3x3	Spr-Fall	White	Med	Green	20	Mod	L-M		Min			•	•			
Rhus ovata Sugar Bush	12x12	Spr	Pink	Med	Green	10	Slow	L-M	•	Min				•	•		
Rosmarinus officinalis Rosemary	4x4	Spr-Fall	Blue, White	Fine	Blue-green	7	Mod	L-M	•	Min		•	•	•	•		
Rosmarinus officinalis prostratus Dwarf Rosemary	2x4	Spr	Blue	Fine	Blue-green	10	Mod	L-M	•	Min		•	•	•			
Ruellia peninsularis Baja Ruellia	4x4	Spr-Fall	Purple	Med	Green	28	Mod	L-M	•	Min			•	•	•		
Salvia chamaedryoides Mexican Blue Sage	2x2	Spr-Fall	Blue	Fine	Gray	15	Mod	L-M	•	Min				•	•		
Salvia clevelandii Chaparral Sage	4x5	Spr	Blue	Fine	Gray green	19	Mod	L-M	•	Min				•	•		
Salvia coccinea Cherry-red Sage	3x2	Spr-Fall	Red	Med	Green	30	Fast	Mod		Min			•	•			

Shrubs

	SIZE	APPEARANCE				LIFE FACTORS				PROBLEMS			LANDSCAPE ZONES				
Botanical Name Common Name	Height x Width (feet)	Flower Season	Flower Color	Foliage Texture	Foliage Color	Hardiness (degrees F)	Growth Rate	Water Use	Evergreen	Litter	Thorns	Allergenic	Mini-oasis	Transition	Arid	Lawn	Revegetation
Salvia farinacea Mealy-cup Sage	1.5x1.5	Spr-Sum	Blue	Med	Green	24-26	Mod	Mod		Min			•	•			
Salvia greggii Autumn Sage	2x2	Spr-Fall	Varies	Fine	Green	0-5	Mod	L-M	•	Min				•	•		
Salvia leucantha Mexican Sage	4x4	Spr & Fall	White, Purple	Med	Gray-green	24-26	Mod	Mod		Min			•	•			
Salvia leucophylla Purple Sage	5x5	Spr	Lav, Pink	Med	Gray	20	Mod	L-M	•	Min				•	•		
Salvia microphylla Baby Salvia	4x5	Spr	Red	Fine	Green	5-10	Mod	L-M	•	Min			•	•	•		
Salvia microphylla 'Sierra Madre'™	4x4	Spr-Fall	Red	Med	Green	5-10	Fast	L-M	•	Min			•	•	•		
Salvia microphylla 'Red Storm'™	3x3	Spr-Fall	Red	Med	Green	5-10	Fast	L-M	•	Min			•	•	•		
Simmondsia chinensis Jojoba	6x6	Spr	N/A	Med	Gray-green	18	Slow	L-M	•	Min				•	•		•
Sophora secundiflora Texas Mt. Laurel, Mescal Bean	15x10	Spr	Purple	Med	Green	0-5	Slow	L-M	•	Min			•	•	•		
Sphaeralcea ambigua Desert Mallow, Globe Mallow	3x3	Spr	Varies	Med	Blue-green	4-5	Fast	L-M	•	Min				•	•		•
Tecoma stans v . angustata Yellow-trumpet Bush, Esperanza	8x8	Spr-Fall	Yellow	Med	Green	28	Fast	L-M	Semi	Mod			•	•	•		
Tecoma stans v. stans Yellow Bells	20x10	Spr-Fall	Yellow	Med	Green	28	Fast	L-M	Semi	Mod			•	•	•		
Vauquelinia californica Arizona Rosewood	15x10	Spr	White	Med	Dark green	5-10	Slow	L-M	•	Min				•	•		
Viguiera stenoloba Skeleton-leaf Goldeneye	3x4	Sum-Fall	Yellow	Fine	Green	5-10	Mod	Low	•	Min			•	•			
Vitex angus-castus Chaste Tree, Monk's Pepper	20x20	Spr	Pink, Lav, White	Med	Sage-green	5-10	Mod	L-M		High			•	•	•	•	
Vitex triangularis Sonoran Vitex	10x10	Spr-Fall	Purple	Med	Sage-green	25	Mod	L-M		Mod			•	•	•		

Groundcovers

Perennials in the desert: two species of verbena intermixed with coral-red yucca contrast with native foothill palo verde and the coarse texture of yellow prickly pear and barrel cactus. Carl Komiskey designed the Engelhard garden in Tucson, Arizona.

Ground covers

Botanical Name / Common Name	SIZE: Height x Width (feet)	APPEARANCE: Flower Season	Flower Color	Foliage Texture	Foliage Color	LIFE FACTORS: Hardiness (degrees F)	Growth Rate	Water Use	Evergreen	PROBLEMS: Litter	Thorns	Allergenic	LANDSCAPE ZONES: Mini-oasis	Transition	Arid	Lawn	Revegetation
Aloe barbadensis (A. vera) Medicinal Aloe	2x2	Spr	Yellow	Coarse	Light green	25	Fast	Low	•	Min	•			•	•		
Aloe saponaria Tiger Aloe	1x1	Spr	Orange	Coarse	Med green	20	Fast	Low	•	Min	•			•	•		
Asparagus densiflorus 'Myers' Foxtail Fern, Myers Asparagus Fern	2x2	Spr-Fall	White	Fine	Green	28	Mod	L-M	•	Min	•			•	•		
Baccharis hybrid 'Centennial' Desert Broom	3x6	Fall	N/A	Fine	Green	15	Fast	L-M	•	Min				•	•		
Baileya multiradiata Desert Marigold	1x1	Spr-Fall	Yellow	Med	Gray	10-15	Mod	Low	•	Min				•	•		•
Bougainvillea brasiliensis Bougainvillea	6x20	Spr-Fall	Varies	Med	Green	32	Fast	L-M	•	Mod	•		•	•	•		
Dalea greggii Trailing Indigo	1x6	Spr	Purple	Fine	Gray	0-5	Fast	L-M	•	Min				•	•		
Dyssodia pentachaeta Golden Fleece, Dahlberg Daisy	.5x.5	Spr-Fall	Yellow	Fine	Green	10	Fast	Low	•	Min				•	•		•
Euphorbia rigida (E. biglandulosa) Euphorbia	2x4	Spr	Chrome Yellow	Med	Gray-green	0	Mod	Low	•	Min				•	•		
Euphorbia myrsinites Euphorbia	.5x1	Spr	Chrome Yellow	Med	Gray-green	<-10	Mod	Low	•	Min				•	•		
Gazania rigens 'Sun Gold' Gazania	.5x1	Spr-Fall	Yellow	Med	Green	20	Mod	Low	•	Min			•	•			
Justicia spicigera Mexican Honeysuckle	3x4	Spr-Fall	Orange	Med	Sage-green	26	Mod	L-M	•	Min			•	•	•		
Lantana montevidensis Trailing Lantana	1x6	Spr-Fall	Purple	Med	Green	32	Fast	L-M		Min			•	•	•		

Ground covers

Botanical Name Common Name	SIZE Height x Width (feet)	APPEARANCE Flower Season	Flower Color	Foliage Texture	Foliage Color	LIFE FACTORS Hardiness (degrees F)	Growth Rate	Water Use	Evergreen	PROBLEMS Litter	Thorns	Allergenic	LANDSCAPE ZONES Mini-oasis	Transition	Arid	Lawn	Revegetation
Melampodium leucanthum Blackfoot Daisy	1x2	Spr-Fall	White	Fine	Gray-green	-5to0	Mod	Low	•	Min				•	•		•
Myoporum parvifolium Trailing Myoporum	1x8	Spr	White	Fine	Green	24	Fast	L-M	•	Min			•	•	•		
Nandina domestica 'Nana' Dwarf Nandina	1x1	Spr	White	Med	Bronze-Green	5-10	Slow	Med	•	Min			•				
Oenothera berlandieri Mexican Evening Primrose	1x3	Spr-Fall	Pink	Fine	Green	24	Fast	Mod	Semi	Min			•	•			
Oenothera caespitosa White Evening Primrose	1x2	Spr-Fall	White	Coarse	Blue-green	10	Mod	L-M	•	Min			•	•	•		•
Oenothera stubbii Saltillo Primrose	.5x1	Spr-Fall	Yellow	Coarse	Green	18-20	Fast	Mod	•	Min			•	•			
Rosmarinus officinalis prostratus Dwarf Rosemary	2x4	Win-Spr	Blue	Fine	Dark green	10	Mod	L-M	•	Min		•	•	•			
Stachys coccinea Scarlet or Texas Betony	1x2	Spr-Fall	Coral	Med	Green	10	Mod	Mod	•	Min			•				•
Verbena gooddingii Goodding Verbena	1x3	Spr	Pink, Lav	Med	Dark green	5	Mod	L-M	•	Min				•	•		•
Verbena peruviana Peruvian Verbena	1x4	Spr-Fall	Varies	Med	Dark green	24	Fast	Mod	•	Min			•	•			
Verbena tenera (V. pulchella v. gracilior) Rock Verbena	1x2	Spr-Fall	Purple, Pink, White	Fine	Dark green	20	Fast	L-M	•	Min			•	•	•		
Verbena rigida Sandpaper Verbena	1x4	Spr-Fall	Purple	Med	Dark green	15	Fast	L-M	•	Min			•	•	•		
Zauschneria californica latifolia California Fuchsia, Hummingbird Trumpet	1x4	Sum-Fall	Red-orange	Med	Sage-green	32	Mod	Mod		Min			•	•			•
Zinnia grandiflora Prairie Zinnia	.5x1	Spr-Fall	Yellow-orange	Fine	Sage-green	10	Mod	L-M	•	Min				•	•		•

Play of color and texture with low-water-use plants. Small water feature provides a reflective quality to enhance plants in this Liebhaber garden in Santa Barbara, California. Designed by Carmen Allison.

Mediterranean fan palm combined with lavender, rosemary and santolina. Shows a mixture of greens and grays complementing the adobe-color home for an overall cool appearance.

Effective use of ground cover using thyme and sedum combined with purple penstemon. Native aspen trees provide a lacy canopy. A beautiful development of outdoor living space gets high color impact with low-water-use plants. Santa Fe, New Mexico. Designed by Ben Haggard of the Well-Tempered Garden.

Accents and Vines

Rosa banksiae 'Lutea'. Lady Bank's Rose

Accents

Botanical Name / Common Name	SIZE: Height x Width (feet)	APPEARANCE: Flower Season	Flower Color	Foliage Texture	Foliage Color	LIFE FACTORS: Hardiness (degrees F)	Growth Rate	Water Use	Evergreen	PROBLEMS: Litter	Thorns	Allergenic	LANDSCAPE ZONES: Mini-oasis	Transition	Arid	Lawn	Revegetation
Agave bovicornuta Cowshorn Agave, Lechuiguilla Verde	4x4	N/A	Yellow	Coarse	Dark green	19	Mod	Low	●	Min	●		●	●	●		
Agave colorata Mescal Ceniza	2x2	Spr	Yellow	Coarse	Gray-green	15	Mod	Low	●	Min	●			●	●		
Agave parryi Parry's Agave	2x2	Sum	Ochre	Coarse	Blue-green	0-5	Slow	Low	●	Min	●			●	●		
Agave vilmoriniana Octopus Agave	4x4	Spr	Yellow	Coarse	Green	15	Mod	Low	●	Min			●	●	●		
Aloe barbadensis (A. vera) Medicinal Aloe	3x3	Spr	Yellow	Coarse	Light green	25	Fast	Low	●	Min	●			●	●		
Aloe saponaria Tiger Aloe	1x1	Spr	Orange	Coarse	Med green	20	Fast	Low	●	Min	●			●	●		
Anigozanthos flavidus Kangaroo Paw	2x2	Spr	Varies	Med	Green	25	Mod	L-M	●	Min			●	●			
Aquilegia chrysantha Golden-spurred Columbine	3x3	Spr-Fall	Yellow	Med	Green	<10	Mod	Mod	●	Min			●				●
Asclepias subulata Desert Milkweed, Ajameta	3x4	Spr-Fall	White	Med	Gray-green	20	Mod	Low	●	Min				●	●		●
Asclepias tuberosa Butterfly Weed	3x3	Sum	Orange	Coarse	Dark green	5	Mod	Low		Min				●	●		
Asparagus densiflorus 'Myers' Foxtail Fern, Myers Asparagus Fern	2x2	Spr-Fall	White	Fine	Green	28	Mod	Mod	●	Min	●		●				
Berlandiera lyrata Chocolate Flower, Lyre Leaf	1x2	Spr-Fall	Yellow	Coarse	Sage-green	10	Mod	Low	●	Min		●	●	●			
Calliandra californica Baja-red Fairy Duster	5x5	Spr-Win	Red	Fine	Dark green	26	Mod	L-M		Min			●	●	●		
Calylophus hartwegii 'Sierra Sundrop'™	2x3	Spr-Fall	Yellow	Med	Light green	5	Mod	Mod	●	Min			●	●			
Cereus hildmannianus Hildmann's Cereus	15x10	Spr-Sum	White	Coarse	Dark green	24	Fast	Low	●	Min	●		●	●	●		
Cycas revoluta Sago Palm	10x5	Spr	Tan	Med	Dark green	15	Slow	L-M	●	Min	●		●				

Accents

Botanical Name Common Name	SIZE Height x Width (feet)	APPEARANCE Flower Season	Flower Color	Foliage Texture	Foliage Color	LIFE FACTORS Hardiness (degrees F)	Growth Rate	Water Use	Evergreen	PROBLEMS Litter	Thorns	Allergenic	LANDSCAPE ZONES Mini-oasis	Transition	Arid	Lawn	Revegetation
Dasylirion acrotriche Green Desert Spoon	4x6	Sum	White	Med	Green	5-10	Slow	Low	•	Min	•			•	•		•
Dasylirion wheeleri Desert Spoon, Sotol	4x6	Sum	White	Med	Blue-green	-5to0	Slow	Low	•	Min	•			•	•		•
Dietes bicolor Evergreen Iris, Fortnight Lily	2x2	Spr-Fall	Yellow	Med	Green	13-18	Mod	Mod	•	Min			•				
Dietes vegeta Evergreen Iris, Fortnight Lily	2x2	Spr-Fall	White	Med	Green	13-18	Mod	Mod	•	Min			•				
Echinocactus grusonii Golden Barrel Cactus	2x4	Spr	Yellow	Coarse	Gold	<18	Slow	Low	•	Min	•			•	•		
Echinocereus engelmannii Hedgehog Cactus	1.5x3	Spr	Pink, Purple	Coarse	Green	<18	Slow	Low	•	Min	•				•		•
Echinopsis multiplex Easter-lily Cactus	1x2	Spr-Sum	Yellow, Pink,Wte	Coarse	Green	19-24	Mod	Low	•	Min	•			•	•		
Ferocactus acanthodes (F. cylindraceus) Compass Barrel	4x2	Spr	Yellow-orange	Coarse	Green	13-18	Slow	Low	•	Min	•			•	•		•
Ferocactus wislizenii Fish-hook Barrel	3x2	Sum-Fall	Yellow, Red	Coarse	Green	0	Slow	Low	•	Min	•			•	•		•
Fouquieria macdougalii Chunari, Ocotillo Macho	10x6	Spr	Red	Med	Green	25	Fast	L-M		Min	•			•			
Hesperaloe funifera Coahuilan Hesperaloe	6x6	Spr	White	Coarse	Blue-green	5-10	Mod	Low	•	Min	•			•	•		
Hesperaloe nocturna Night-flowering Hesperaloe	4x4	Spr	White	Coarse	Blue-green	10-15	Mod	Low	•	Min	•			•	•		
Hesperaloe parviflora Red Yucca, Hesperaloe	3x3	Spr-Fall	Coral	Med	Blue-green	-5-0	Mod	Low	•	Min			•	•	•		
Ipomea carnea v. fistulosa Diez en la Mañana	10x6	Sum-Fall	Laven-der	Coarse	Green	30	Fast	Mod		L-M			•				
Lophocereus schottii forma monstrosus Totem Pole Cactus	10x4	Spr	Pink	Coarse	Green	19-24	Slow	Low	•	Min				•	•		

Accents

Botanical Name / Common Name	SIZE	APPEARANCE				LIFE FACTORS				PROBLEMS			LANDSCAPE ZONES				
	Height x Width (feet)	Flower Season	Flower Color	Foliage Texture	Foliage Color	Hardiness (degrees F)	Growth Rate	Water Use	Evergreen	Litter	Thorns	Allergenic	Mini-oasis	Transition	Arid	Lawn	Revegetation
Lotus rigidus Deer Vetch	3x3	Spr	Yellow	Fine	Green	<18	Mod	Min	•	Min				•	•		•
Melampodium leucanthum Blackfoot Daisy	1x2	Spr-Fall	White	Fine	Gray-green	-5to0	Mod	Low	•	Min				•	•		•
Muhlenbergia dumosa Bamboo Muhly	4x3	April	Tan	Fine	Green	20	Fast	Mod	•	Min			•	•			
Muhlenbergia emersleyi Bull Grass	5x5	Fall	Cream	Med	Green	5-10	Mod	Mod	•	Min				•	•		•
Muhlenbergia lindheimeri Lindheimer Muhly	4x4	Fall	Silver	Fine	Blue-green	5-10	Mod	Mod	•	Min				•	•		•
Muhlenbergia rigens Deer Grass	4x4	Fall	Brown	Fine	Green	15	Fast	Mod	•	Min			•	•	•		•
Opuntia acanthocarpa Buckhorn Cholla	5x5	Spr	Varies	Coarse	Green	19-24	Mod	Low	•	Min	•			•	•		•
Opuntia basilaris Beavertail Prickly Pear	1x4	Spr	Fuchsia	Coarse	Light blue-grn	10	Slow	Low	•	Min	•			•	•		•
Opuntia leptocaulis Desert Christmas Cholla	3x3	Spr	Yellow	Med	Light green	0	Mod	Low	•	Min	•			•	•		•
Opuntia phaecantha v. discata (O. engelmannii) Engelmann's Prickly Pear	3x4	Spr	Yellow	Coarse	Light green	10	Mod	Low	•	Min	•			•	•		•
Opuntia robusta Prickly Pear	10x10	Spr	Yellow	Coarse	Light green	<15	Mod	Low	•	Min	•			•	•		•
Opuntia violacea santa-rita Purple Prickly Pear	3x4	Spr	Yellow	Coarse	Purple	15	Mod	Low	•	Min	•			•	•		•
Pachycereus (Stenocereus) marginatus Mexican Organ Pipe	10x10	Spr	Pink	Coarse	Dark green	20	Fast	Low	•	Min	•			•	•		
Penstemon baccharifolius 'Del Rio'™ Rock Penstemon	1.5x1.5	Sum	Red	Med	Green	5	Mod	Mod	•	Min				•	•		
Penstemon barbatus Scarlet Bugler	2x1	Sum	Red	Med	Gray-green	0	Mod	Mod	•	Min				•	•		
Penstemon eatonii Firecracker Penstemon	2x2	Spr	Red	Med	Green	10-15	Mod	Low	•	Min				•	•		•

Accents

Botanical Name / Common Name	Height x Width (feet)	Flower Season	Flower Color	Foliage Texture	Foliage Color	Hardiness (degrees F)	Growth Rate	Water Use	Evergreen	Litter	Thorns	Allergenic	Mini-oasis	Transition	Arid	Lawn	Revegetation
	SIZE	**APPEARANCE**				**LIFE FACTORS**				**PROBLEMS**			**LANDSCAPE ZONES**				
Penstemon fendleri Fendler's Penstemon	1x1	Spr	Laven-der	Med	Gray-green	0	Mod	Mod	•	Min				•	•		
Penstemon palmeri Palmer's Penstemon	3x4	Spr	Light Pink	Med	Blue-green	0	Mod	Low	•	Min				•	•		•
Penstemon parryi Parry's Penstemon	2x2	Spr	Hot Pink	Med	Blue-green	15	Mod	Low	•	Min				•	•		•
Penstemon pseudospectabilis Canyon Penstemon	5x2	Spr	Fuchsia	Med	Blue-green	10	Mod	Mod	•	Min				•	•		•
Penstemon spectabilis Royal Penstemon	2x2	Spr	Blue	Med	Green	10-15	Mod	Low	•	Min				•	•		•
Penstemon superbus Superb Penstemon	2x2	Spr	Coral	Med	Blue-green	5-10	Mod	Low	•	Min				•	•		•
Penstemon thurberi Thurber's Penstemon	1.5x1.5	Spr-Sum	Laven-der	Fine	Green	5-10	Mod	Low	•	Min				•	•		
Penstemon wrightii Wright's Penstemon	3x3	Spr-Fall	Pink-Rose	Large	Light green	5-10	Mod	Low	•	Min				•	•		
Phoenix roebelenii Pigmy Date Palm	8x4	N/A	N/A	Fine	Green	25	Slow	Mod	•	Min	•		•				
Psilostrophe cooperi Paper Flower	1.5x2	Spr-Fall	Yellow	Med	Green	5-10	Mod	L-M	•	Min				•	•		•
Psilostrophe tagetina Paper Flower	1.5x2	Sum	Yellow	Fine	Green	0-5	Mod	L-M	•	Min			•	•	•		•
Rosmarinus officinalis Rosemary	4x4	Spr	Blue	Fine	Dark green	7	Mod	L-M	•	Min			•	•	•		
Sphaeralcea ambigua Globe Mallow, Desert Mallow	3x3	Spr	Varies	Med	Blue-green	4-5	Fast	Mod	•	Min				•	•		•
Tagates palmeri (lemmoni) Mountain Marigold	5x5	Fall	Yellow	Med	Green	30	Mod	Mod		Min		•	•	•			
Tagates lucida Mexican Tarragon, Mt. Atlas Anise	3x2	Fall	Yellow	Med	Green	32	Fast	Mod		Min			•	•			
Trichocereus candicans	2x3	Spr-Sum	White	Coarse	Green	10	Mod	Low	•	Min	•		•	•			
Trichocereus huascha hyb.	2x3	Spr-Sum	Red, Fuchsia	Coarse	Green	10	Mod	Low	•	Min	•		•	•			

Accents & Vines

Botanical Name / Common Name	SIZE: Height x Width (feet)	APPEARANCE: Flower Season	Flower Color	Foliage Texture	Foliage Color	LIFE FACTORS: Hardiness (degrees F)	Growth Rate	Water Use	Evergreen	PROBLEMS: Litter	Thorns	Allergenic	LANDSCAPE ZONES: Mini-oasis	Transition	Arid	Lawn	Revegetation
Yucca aloifolia Spanish Bayonet	10x10	Spr	White	Coarse	Green	9-18	Mod	Low	•	Min	•			•	•		
Yucca baccata Banana Yucca	3x6	Spr	White	Coarse	Green	5-10	Slow	Low	•	Min	•			•	•		•
Yucca elata Soap-tree Yucca	20x10	Spr	White	Med	Blue-green	-5to0	Slow	Low	•	Min				•	•		•
Yucca recurvifolia Pendulous Yucca	6x6	Spr& Fall	White	Med	Blue-green	5-9	Mod	L-M	•	Min			•	•	•		
Yucca rigida Blue Yucca	8x3	Spr	White	Med	Blue	10	Slow	Low	•	Min	•			•	•		•
Yucca rostrata Beard Yucca	12x5	Spr	White	Coarse	Blue	5	Slow	Low	•	Min	•			•	•		•
Antigonon leptopus Coral Vine, Queen's Wreath, San Miguelito	40x20	Sum-Fall	Rose, White, Pink	Coarse	Green	30	Fast	Mod		Mod			•	•			
Bougainvillea brasiliensis Bougainvillea	20x10	Spr-Fall	Varies	Med	Green	32	Fast	Low	•	Mod	•		•	•	•		
Macfadyena unguis-cati Cat's-claw Vine	20x15	Spr	Yellow	Med	Green	13-18	Fast	L-M	•	Mod			•	•	•		
Mascagnia lilacina Lavender Orchid Vine	15x10	Sum	Lavender	Med	Green	15-18	Fast	L-M		Mod			•	•	•		
Mascagnia macroptera Yellow Orchid Vine	15x10	Sum	Yellow	Med	Green	24	Fast	L-M		Mod			•	•	•		
Merremia aurea Yellow Morning Glory	15x10	Sum	Yellow	Fine	Green	26	Fast	L-M		Mod			•	•	•		
Podranea ricasoliana Pink-trumpet Vine	20x10	Sum-Fall	Pink	Med	Green	26	Fast	L-M		Mod			•	•			
Rosa banksiae 'Alba plena' White Lady Bank's Rose	20x15	Spr	White	Med	Green	10	Fast	Mod	•	Mod	•		•	•			
Rosa banksiae 'Lutea' Yellow Lady Bank's Rose	20x15	Spr	Yellow	Med	Green	10	Fast	Mod	•	Mod			•	•			
Tecoma stans v. angustata Yellow-trumpet Bush, Esperanza	8x8	Spr-Fall	Yellow	Med	Green	28	Fast	L-M	Semi	Mod			•	•	•		
Tecoma stans v. stans Yellow Bells	20x10	Spr-Fall	Yellow	Med	Green	28	Fast	L-M	Semi	Mod			•	•	•		

Horticulture

A variety of foliage colors and textures creates an interesting, yet tranquil, garden. Isabel Green design, Santa Barbara, California.

Horticulture

Successful gardeners know something about *horticulture*, the science of growing plants. This chapter provides a framework of sound horticultural principles that you can use to plant, grow and maintain the plants you select. The information is easy to understand.

Photo above: Kangaroo Paw, Blue Fescue and Aeoniums are used in combination with river cobble and flagstone to create a pleasing appearance. This is true low-water-use and low-maintenance.

Although this chapter is placed at the end, the next few pages encompass the most important part of this book. If you're like most people, you look at the pictures first when you pick up a plant or gardening book. But after selecting a variety of plants that you like, you have to figure out what to do with them. Can they fit into your landscape? What about irrigation? How much water does a low-water-use plant need? What is a low-water-use plant?

Included in this chapter are: the principles behind an environmentally-sensitive landscape; guidelines for purchasing and planting; explanation of an efficient irrigation system; watering schedules; and a checklist for detecting drought stress in plants.

Xeriscape Principles

The seven fundamental Xeriscape™ principles that follow are the same for any site.

Planning and Design

Good planning is the first and most important principle. Whether through professional help or individual research, you need to determine the relationship between landscaping and living areas and make plans to reduce the heat, harvest runoff water, and possibly allow for construction and installation in phases.

The first step is site analysis. Start by sketching the area to be designed, then evaluate existing conditions. Make notes directly on your plan showing the house on the lot. Among things to consider are: good and bad views, prevailing wind direction, the location of utilities (including overhead wires), existing plants and structures, rock outcroppings, drainage, the angle of the sun, etc. Use these factors to determine how you will use each area. Identify areas needing shade.

Writing a wish list is the second planning step. Simply list the features you desire in your garden. Also list areas which are unsatisfactory. Organize items on your list into categories such as entry, main patio, etc.

Careful landscape planning is necessary to help keep a home cool in the summer and warm in the winter and to improve energy efficiency.

In summer, the east and west exposures of a building have the greatest heat gain. The warmer the climate, the more important shade is in these areas. The greatest heat gain in winter is on the south and southwest sides. In colder areas, it is important to maximize this heat gain. Outdoor-living areas need similar considerations if they are to be used comfortably year-round.

Remember that subdivisions are usually planned to provide the maximum quantity of lots on a parcel of land. As a result, production housing (tract housing) is oriented to maximize the developer's profit, not to improve energy efficiency.

As you determine how to use each area, consider the functional and visual relationship of interior to exterior space. Provide safe and efficient pathways.

If traffic patterns and lines of vision are kept free of clutter, both indoor and outdoor areas will seem more spacious. Enhance this effect by using the same type or color of flooring throughout the interior-to-exterior transition.

Don't forget to provide for practical things such as a place for garbage cans and bicycle storage. Night lighting must be provided for safety. Consider any special needs of small children and the elderly.

During the planning process, you will also want to consider where you might need shade or screening for privacy. In each case, decide whether plants or a structural element — such as a ramada or wall — would work better.

Another safety consideration is pool placement and enclosure. Many communities require a pool fence in addition to backyard fencing on the property line. The additional protection should help reduce the number of child drownings.

FIGURE 3: ***Typical Landscape Zones.*** *For greatest water-use efficiency, separate the landscape into three zones: mini-oasis, transition and arid.*

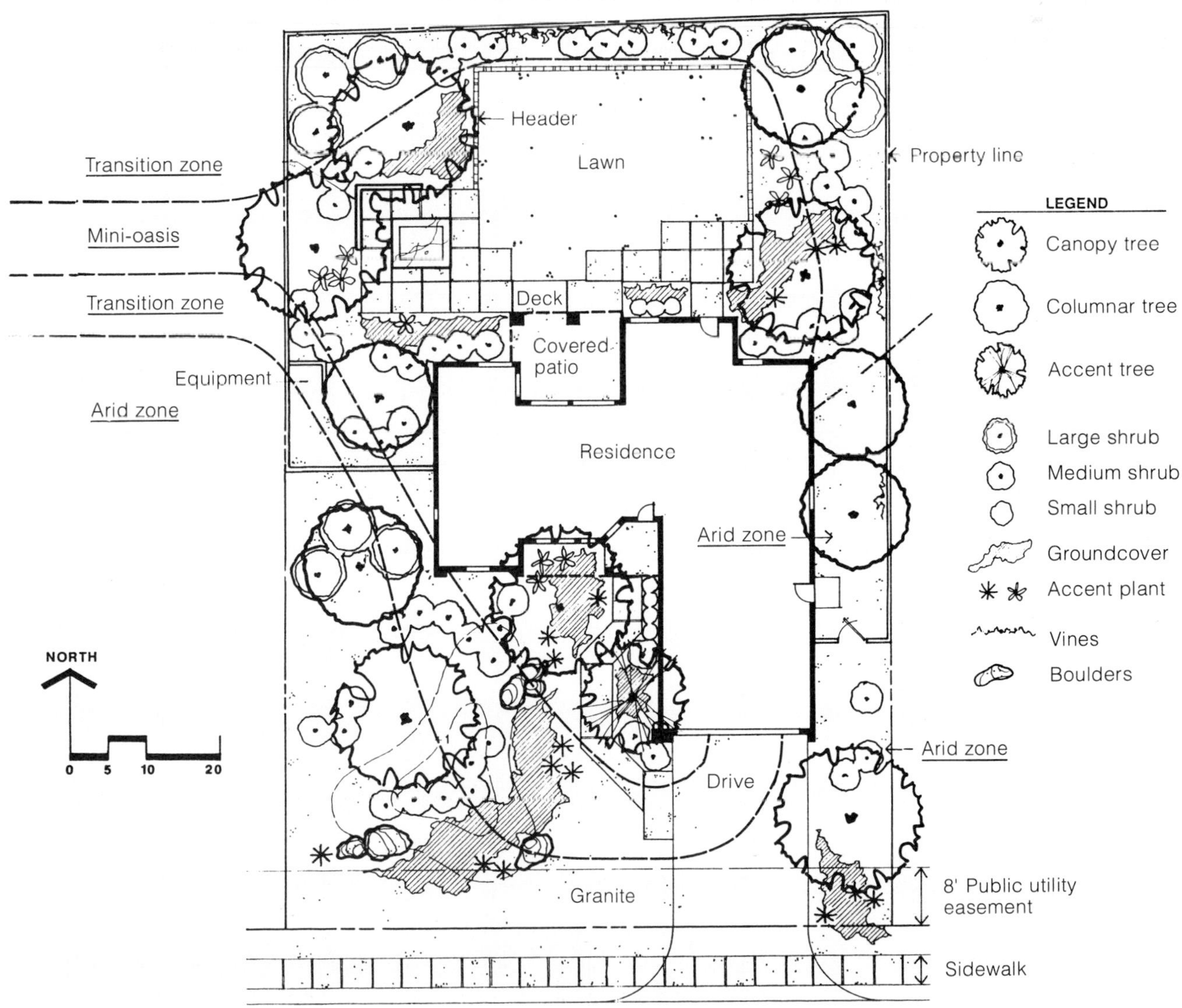

Properly planted and irrigated low-water-use groundcover can reduce water use by 90 percent.

Draw your house and lot on graph paper with 1/8-inch squares. Each square will equal 1 foot. Locate all windows, doors and permanent fixtures such as water meter, electric meter, electric service, gas meter, etc. Make several copies. Use one for your site analysis. Use the others to experiment with design alternatives.

Make your backyard accessible from the house without going through the pool enclosure.

For greatest water-use efficiency, separate the landscape into three zones: mini-oasis, transition and arid. Place plants that use the most water adjacent to outdoor living areas where they can be most appreciated and provide cooling. Determine the extent and boundaries of the mini-oasis surrounding the outdoor living areas as well as the extent of the transition and arid zones. Where will each zone start and stop?

Buildings and hardscape, such as patios, make a significant portion of any site impermeable to water infiltration. They also generate the greatest runoff. With proper planning, this stormwater runoff can be used in a mini-oasis zone, the zone generally adjacent to buildings and patios.

In arid and semiarid areas, it is important to keep as much rainfall as possible on the land. Although rainfall may not be sufficient for regular irrigation needs, it can help encourage deep roots and leach salts. Consider the type of soil on your lot, however, and be sure to provide an overflow outlet.

If one-half of a site receiving an average annual rainfall of 6 inches is impermeable, the remaining one-half absorbs double that or 12 inches of rainfall. If three-quarters of the site is impermeable, the remaining one-quarter has 2 feet of rainfall available.

Should budgetary constraints require you to landscape in phases, a well-developed plan will help avoid conflicts. Set priorities based on personal needs and available dollars. Because trees have the greatest visual and environmental impact, give them high priority.

Practical Turf Areas

It is estimated that nearly one-quarter of all water consumed in a household goes toward maintaining a lawn. To help offset this consumption, limit turf to areas needed for active recreation. An area 20' x 30' is sufficient for family volleyball. Turf is the highest maintenance area in any landscape.

Minimizing turf area reduces water use, the personal energy necessary for maintenance and green waste. Low-growing groundcovers can provide a lush look where active recreation is neither desired nor possible.

The following comparison between lawn and Myoporum, a groundcover discussed on page 62, (and the subsequent water savings) offers a remarkable statement on the environmental benefits of using low-water-use plants.

In Phoenix, Arizona the most dramatic comparison can be made for peak summer conditions in June. During this month, experts recommend that you apply 2.5 inches of water per week on a lawn.

Assuming your lawn area is 1,000 square feet, 1,558 gallons would be needed per week to follow this guideline and keep your lawn green. (After the monsoons start, it may take only 2 inches per week for a total weekly usage of 1,246 gallons —a difference of over 300 gallons per week from month to month.)

Covering the same 1,000-square-foot area with a soft, green, arid-region groundcover such as Myoporum would require about 28 plants placed 6-feet apart. Using drip irrigation programmed to provide three gallons of water to each plant two times a week would use only 168 gallons per week, which is adequate for Myoporum throughout the summer.

Based on this example, we can conclude that this lawn will consume between 1,178 and 1,490 more gallons per week than a common groundcover. To help visualize how much water this is, consider that the average home spa holds less than 500 gallons.

Low-water-use groundcovers provide cooling in the same way grass does. When combined with trees that shade the house, energy savings are realized.

The choice is clear: Native- and arid-region low-water-use plants can have a tremendous impact on improving the year-round appearance of your landscape without draining your natural resources. These plant choices, properly watered, will last for years. They will also save your financial resources through reduced water, maintenance and replacement costs.

Efficient Irrigation

An efficient irrigation system is essential for proper water management and plant development. A 1991 study by the City of Phoenix reported that approximately 40 percent of the homes there have an irrigation system. A similar percentage probably holds true for other southwestern cities.

The most cost-effective action homeowners can take is to install a properly designed irrigation system in their existing landscape. Older landscapes with irrigation systems can benefit from new controllers and conversion to drip for shrub and groundcover areas.

Although more costly, a major landscape renovation using Xeriscape principles provides long-term environmental benefits. More on irrigation later.

Analysis and Soil Amendments

Soil amendments such as forest mulch and soil sulfur can improve the water-holding capacity of the soil and provide nutrients which benefit plant growth. Be sure to select nitrogen-stabilized forest-mulch products. Avoid products containing redwood. For best results, add the amendments during the planting process.

Plants native to your area can survive in the native soil. Aside from environmental issues, this is the best argument for using native plants. However, under the most severe conditions even native plants may perform poorly. Contact your local agricultural extension service to learn more about the specific soil type on your property. They will be able to advise you regarding the best selection of amendments.

Mulch

Mulch is applied over the soil to provide shade to cool the soil and to reduce evaporation of moisture from the soil. Other benefits can be a cooler root zone and reduced erosion and weed growth.

Mulch can be organic — from plants — or inorganic — rock or gravel. Organic mulches are best when mixed into the top several inches of soil so they won't blow away. Mulches should be applied 2-6" deep.

Appropriate Plants

Incorporating low-water-use plants in the landscape is a major step toward reducing landscape-water use.

The definition of low-water-use plants varies for each region. Generally, the water required by plants native to a region — or from other regions with similar climate and soils — matches the amount of water available. Conceivably those plants can exist on rainfall once they are established.

In order to maintain aesthetics, however, most plants need supplemental water at least in summer. Variations in local temperatures, humidity, rainfall, wind and soil type will vary the water needs of plants.

Plants from the driest portions of arid regions tend to have small leaves, thereby lowering leaf temperature and water loss through transpiration. Other plants defoliate during dry seasons to avoid drought. Incorporating arid-region plants in the landscape and employing proper mulching techniques minimizes evapotranspiration. (See Figure 4)

Although low-water-use plants can fulfill all landscape needs, it's OK to succumb to a passion for roses or other thirsty imports in a moderate way. Plant them near the outdoor living area or mini-oasis and use an abundance of soil improvements and mulches. After studying the plants in this book you may develop a passion for arid beauties instead.

Because trees have the greatest visual and environmental impact, give them high priority. Appropriately selected and positioned trees will greatly reduce cooling costs in the summer.

Following the Xeriscape principles will reduce landscape maintenance.

Maintenance

The seventh and final Xeriscape principle is appropriate maintenance. Maintenance includes: pruning, weeding, fertilization, insect control, irrigation — everything involved in plant care. Pruning and irrigation are the areas in which appropriate procedures are most often violated. Unless you're working on an espalier or topiary (a bush pruned to look like a Disney character or some other figure), plants should be allowed to grow in their natural form — not trimmed into cubes or spheres.

Once a plant is sheared, it has to be kept up and turf has to be mowed regularly. For these reasons most landscapes are high maintenance. A natural approach can reduce your maintenance time by 90 percent. Instead of shearing shrubs, use your time better by properly thinning trees to prevent wind damage.

Several publishers produce excellent pruning guides in paperback. Purchase and read one. Save severe pruning for the cool season to prevent sunburn of interior branches. Lightly prune flowering plants just following the bloom period so buds won't be removed.

Proper plant selection and placement will greatly reduce maintenance. Plants adapted to local climate and soil conditions will outperform species needing continuous supplements. Place plants so they have room to grow to mature size. When placed inappropriately they may overgrow gates, walks or windows. As a result, constant pruning is needed or the plant has to be removed.

Appropriate maintenance includes frequent visual checking of the irrigation system for proper operation. Automatic controllers are usually set to operate either when we're asleep or at work. So, run each of the stations manually and make certain all plants are getting water. Also look for leaks; plant foliage inhibiting turf sprays; broken, missing, or clogged irrigation heads; and emitters that need to be temporarily capped.

Automatic controllers can waste water if they're not adjusted whenever there is a subtle change in the weather. Guidelines for scheduling are discussed in the following section on irrigation. No landscape design can reach its potential without proper maintenance.

FIGURE 4: ***The Process of Evapotranspiration.***

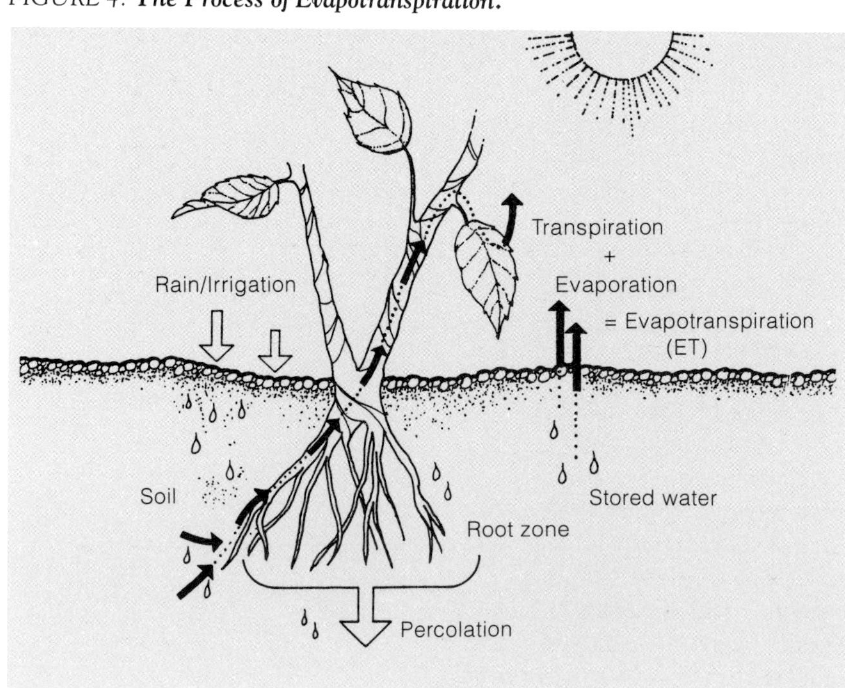

Planting

Year-round planting is practical in the lower elevations of the southwestern United States. Frost-sensitive plants such as citrus and Bougainvillea should not be installed from September through the latest date of local frost.

For all other plants there are several advantages to planting in the fall: 1. Lower temperatures reduce stress on plants. 2. Less water is needed for establishment. 3. Root development continues through winter. The established root system can support vigorous foliage growth in spring. 4. Plants are reasonably established by the time the heat hits and will be more drought-tolerant.

If your property is ready for landscaping in late spring, don't spend the summer in a "zeroscape."

Go ahead and plant. Just be sure the irrigation system is installed prior to planting and closely monitor the condition of the plants.

Use the following steps as a guide when planting:

Select Your Plants

Once the basic design is laid out, you can begin selecting plants. When placing and selecting trees, consider which size and form is most appropriate. Some trees grow in an upright form. Others form an umbrella or canopy shape.

Size is equally important. Trees with a small mature height can be squeezed into tight spaces. Large trees need lots of space. They will not meet your expectations for performance when cramped. When large trees with aggressive root systems are squeezed into small spaces, they may damage plumbing, buildings or other structural elements.

Graceful branch patterns can relieve a blank wall. Shadow patterns add interest to walls and pavement. Use a deciduous rather than an evergreen tree in places where you want the warmth of the sun in winter. Near pools, spas, fountains and ponds use only the most litter-free trees. Use a groundcover with an open, spreading growth habit under trees which litter heavily to conceal the litter and reduce maintenance.

When placing shrubs, allow for their mature size. It may take the shrubs 2-3 years to reach full size and the landscape may appear somewhat sparse at first. By spacing shrubs properly, you will reduce the initial cost of plants and irrigation as well as maintenance costs over the years.

Grouping plants with highly contrasting foliage color and texture creates an enhanced effect. The foliage alone will be interesting.

With careful plant selection, flower color is possible nearly year-round. A general color scheme can be maintained if desired, or have fun changing colors through the year.

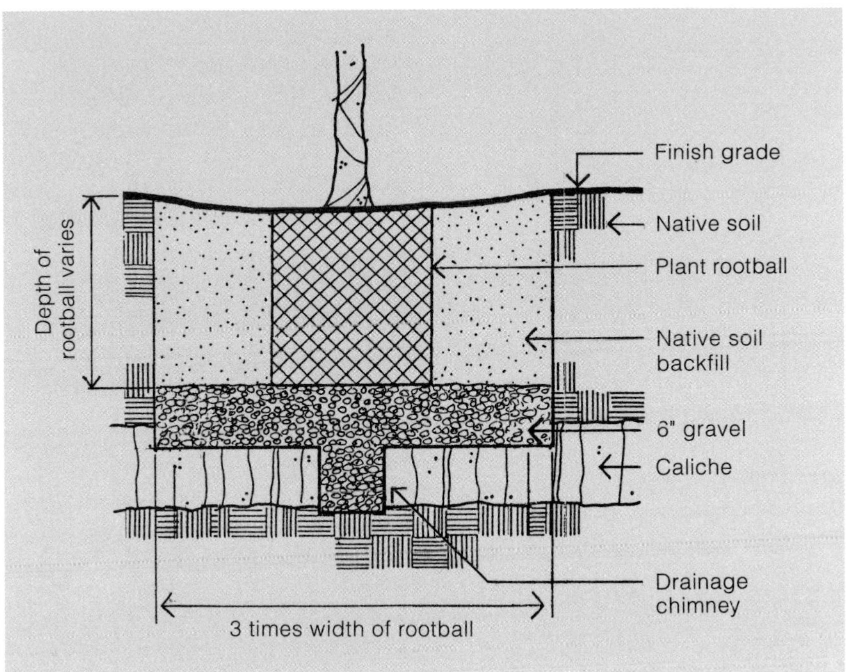

FIGURE 5: ***Planting in Caliche.*** *In areas with caliche, the addition of soil sulfur and organic matter to the backfill will help to break down the caliche and release nutrients to the plants. 6 inches of gravel is used atop the caliche. The rootball is placed on top of the gravel.*

Install Irrigation System

Install the entire irrigation system prior to planting. Check controller, valves, emitters, etc. for proper operation. Make any needed repairs before you begin planting.

Don't install plants until after the irrigation system is completed.

Moisten the Soil

Get some moisture into the soil by operating the irrigation system. This makes digging plant pits easier and keeps dry soil around the plant pits from drawing water away from the rootball.

In general, plan to use 1-gallon-size or larger groundcover, vines or accent plants. Anything smaller does not have enough root structure. Plants smaller than 1-gallon are too delicate and will suffer a high rate of loss.

Buy shrubs in 1-gallon or 5-gallon sizes.

Trees can be 5-gallon, 15-gallon or 24-inch-box size. 5-gallon trees establish more quickly and with less loss, but will take an additional year to get to the same size as a 15-gallon tree. Over a 2-year period, a 15-gallon tree and a 24-inch-box tree will usually grow to the same size.

Dig Plant Pits

Dig plant pits three times the diameter and equal to height of the rootball. In areas with caliche, dig through the caliche for proper drainage. (See Figure 5)

Fill the pit with water and observe how fast it drains out. If water is still there several hours later, you have more digging to do. A pickaxe and a crowbar or a caliche bar may be required. Better yet, hire someone with a backhoe or jackhammer and get them to do this tough work. Don't waste your money

New concepts for plant pits are illustrated in Figures 5, 6, 7.

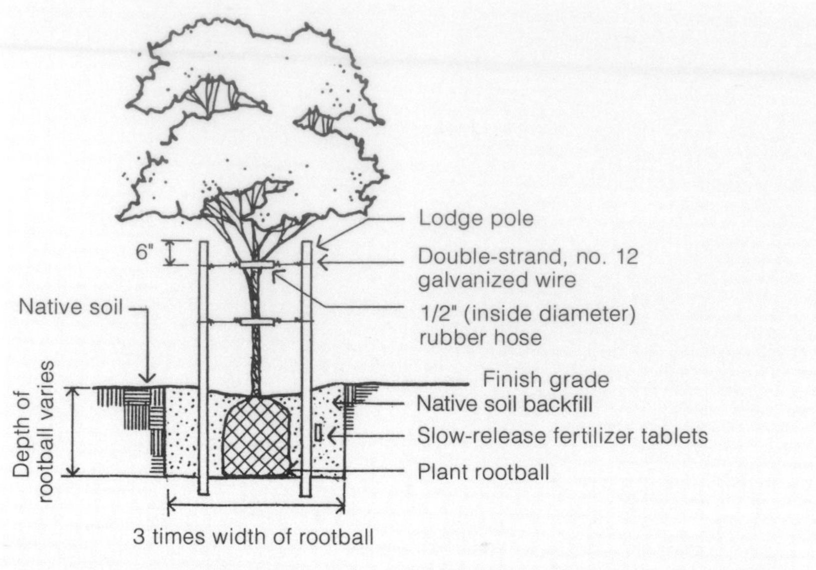

FIGURE 6: **Tree Planting.** *Lodge pole height will vary. For maximum support, place top tie above lowest scaffold branches, bottom tie halfway between top tie and grade or ground level. The rootball is placed on top of the native soil.*

FIGURE 7: **Shrub Planting.** *Note that the rootball is placed on top of the native soil.*

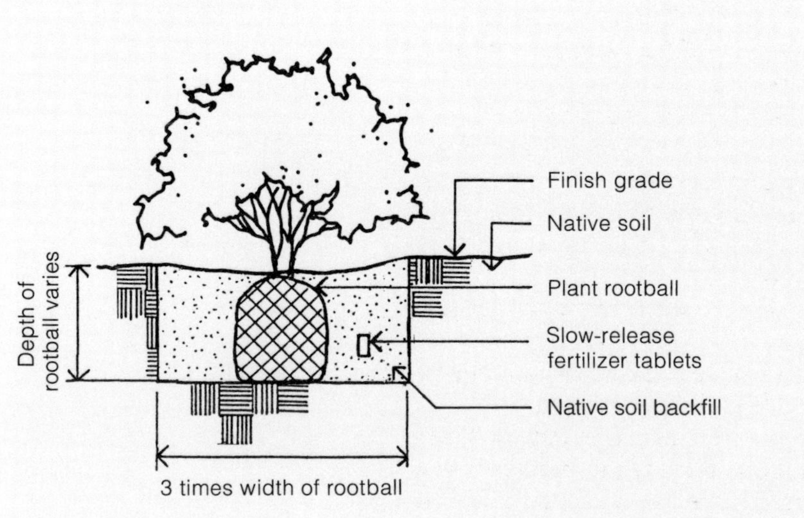

on products advertised as caliche-dissolvers or caliche busters. They don't work!

Purchase Your Plants

It is a good idea to place an order with your favorite retail nursery several weeks before you need the plants. Partial payment may be required as a deposit. Wait to purchase them until you are really ready to put them in the ground. This will allow the nursery time to locate any species they don't normally carry and have them shipped in, thus guaranteeing that correct quantities will be found.

Don't accept any plants that do not appear to be healthy and well-formed. It is also not a good idea to select plants which are oversized for their container. They may have been in the container too long and developed root problems. Choose moderate-size plants with balanced shape. Many native plants dislike being grown in containers and will not appear to be robust.

When selecting trees look for higher-branching individuals for placement near walks, streets, drives and patios. Ask to have the plants delivered in staged shipments — trees first, then shrubs and, lastly, groundcover.

Take Care of Rootballs

Once the plants are delivered they are your responsibility. Immediately water any plants that appear to be dry. Check the soil in the container. Thorough daily watering of the container is necessary until planting. During the heat of the summer, watering twice daily may be necessary.

If the rootball has separated from the wall of the container, push soil into the crack so the rootball can be properly watered.

To remove plants from plastic containers, lay the container on its side. Gently roll the container while pressing on the side. This will loosen the rootball from the container wall. With smaller containers, tip the plant upside down onto one hand and pull off the container with the other. Use both hands to position the plant in the planting hole.

The last part of this technique doesn't work with trees. Tip the tree onto its side. After rolling the container and pressing the sides—with the tree still on its side—have someone tilt the bottom of the container a few inches while you gently pull the trunk. If the rootball doesn't come out easily, roll and press the container some more. Pulling too hard will destroy the root system and kill the tree. It may be necessary to cut the sides of the container to free the rootball. You may need a helper when planting 15-gallon-size trees. Place the rootball in the planting hole; backfill and water immediately. Fill in as necessary to top of rootball. Boxed trees should be placed in the planting hole. Then remove the sides. Leave the box bottom in the hole.

Backfill
Plants properly suited to the local soils will perform well with native soil as the backfill. In areas with caliche, the addition of soil sulfur and organic matter to the backfill will help to break down the caliche and release nutrients to the plants. Although it is often recommended, gypsum should not be used because it is ineffective in caliche or calcified soils.

The water-holding capacity of sandy soil is improved with the addition of organic matter such as nitrogen-stabilized forest humus. Use no more than one part humus to two parts soil. Do not use redwood soil amendments. Tamp soil while backfilling to eliminate air pockets. Water with irrigation system or hose to settle soil. Add more soil in areas that sink to bring the level to the top of the rootball.

Mulch
Mulch surface with rock, gravel or organic material. Fine-textured mulch such as forest humus stays in place best when incorporated into the top 4 - 6" of soil.

Adjust Emitters
If necessary, adjust emitter location and height. (See Figure 10) On slopes, the emitter must be uphill from rootball.

Stake the Trees
Only stake trees that were staked in the nursery containers. Don't tie trunk and branches tightly. They need to move to develop strength. (See Figure 8)

Prune
Prune lightly to shape the plant form and remove crossing or broken branches.

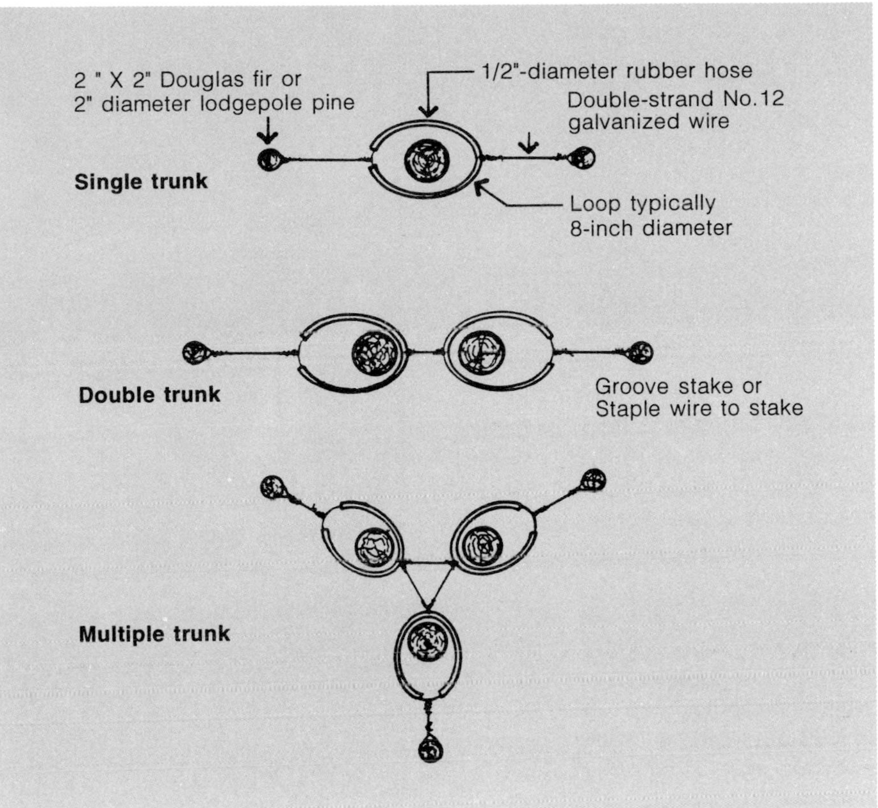

FIGURE 8: ***Tree Staking.*** *Stake trees that were staked in the nursery containers. Don't tie trunk and branches tightly. Multi-trunk trees must have all major leaders staked or supported.*

Irrigation

A well-designed irrigation system provides the tools for efficient water management in the landscape. There is a lot of hardware available to serve the wide variety of watering needs found in landscapes. Figuring out what you need can be confusing. The following information will help you match appropriate hardware to your water needs.

It is best to purchase irrigation equipment from an irrigation-supply house or distributor rather than a do-it-yourself hardware store. Staff at the irrigation supply house can advise you. They also carry better-quality materials and will usually maintain a stock of repair parts to fit what you have purchased. Doing it right will save time, money and aggravation.

There are varying water needs within a landscape. Each need creates a separate zone which must be valved separately on the irrigation system. This way each area can be watered at the frequency and duration needed to maintain healthy plants.

North, south, east and west exposures adjacent to buildings are shaded by the structure for various portions of the day thereby varying the sun exposure for each orientation. Areas receiving full sun all day should be separate from these zones.

Other possible zones are: turf areas, specialty plantings such as roses or wildflowers, seasonal flowers, fruit trees, the landscape zones (mini-oasis, transition and arid), an herb or vegetable garden, potted plants, and embankments.

Figure 9 is a schematic illustration of the relationship of each component of an irrigation system to the others. Following is a discussion of irrigation-system components and their functions.

Mainline

The irrigation mainline carries water from the source to all valves in the system. The mainline can be cut into the water-service line anywhere between the meter and building.

Vacuum Breaker

The vacuum breaker separates the irrigation system from the water used indoors. It prohibits insects and chemicals that may enter the irrigation system from contaminating the potable water. Place the vacuum breaker in the mainline near the connection with the water service. This equipment is above grade and should be located where it can be screened with plants. Although a reduced-pressure-type vacuum breaker is usually required, check local codes for other requirements. All irrigation valves will be placed downstream from the vacuum breaker.

Vacuum breakers require regular maintenance. The wye strainer, which catches debris in the line, should be flushed quarterly. Any leaks should be repaired at once. Some communities require regular testing by certified companies for proper operation. Most cities require a permit to ensure proper installation. Be sure to find out local requirements.

Controller

An irrigation system can be operated manually or by electric controllers. An electric controller operates the system more efficiently than manual operation if it is reprogrammed for seasonal weather changes. Other advantages of the automatic system include: operation at night when water pressure is highest and evaporation lowest and reduction of time required for manual maintenance.

A manual system requires attention through the duration of the watering cycle to turn valves on and off. Some valves may run longer than necessary. Others may be forgotten. This is wasteful and plant performance will not be ideal.

Several manufacturers produce good quality microprocessor controllers. Some are easier to operate

FIGURE 9: **Irrigation Schematic.** *A schematic illustration of the relationship of each irrigation-system component to the others.*

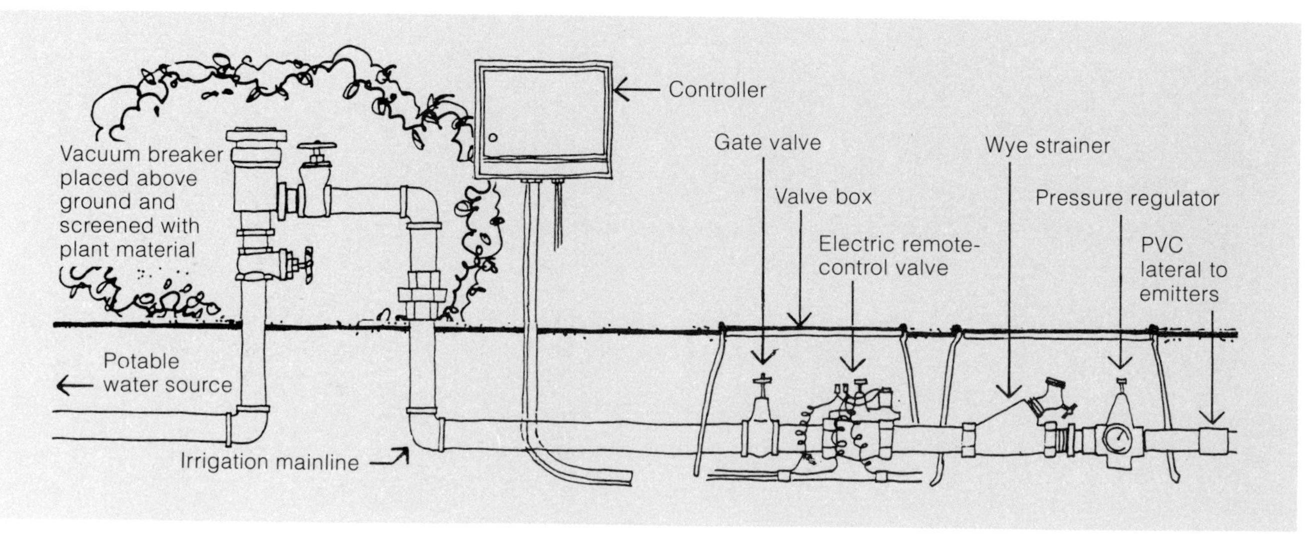

than others. So look them over carefully for ease of operation and features. These controllers are quite trouble-free and extremely accurate.

Almost every landscape needs at least a dual-program controller. This allows two different watering schedules such as: lawn watering at frequent intervals and for short duration; or drip irrigation at infrequent intervals and for long duration. All valves on either program will have to run on the same days. Only the duration for each can vary.

If additional programs are needed on a small project (most residential property), it is most cost effective to add another dual-program controller rather than purchasing a large controller with more stations.

The operator must be careful to program the controllers so only one valve is running at a time. Trying to run more than one valve at a time may reduce water pressure so much that indoor use is unacceptable. If you feel juggling water schedules among several controllers is too bothersome, then buy the larger controller.

Controllers are available that program each valve independently. For example: 16 valves equal 16 programs. This flexibility is ideal for large residences or small commercial projects with a wide variety of watering needs.

Hint: Older irrigation systems can be made much more efficient by exchanging the existing controller for a newer microprocessor controller.

Valves

Valves turn irrigation in the various zones on and off. They may be constructed from brass or plastic. Different types of valves are required for high-volume lawn sprays versus extremely low-volume drip irrigation. All valves should be placed below grade (below ground level) in irrigation-valve boxes for aesthetics and to protect them from ultraviolet rays and vandalism. Install only one valve per box. If you crowd two into a box it is nearly impossible to maintain them.

Space valves a minimum of 16" apart so the boxes will fit over them. For drip systems, the wye strainer and pressure regulator need to be in a box too. Wiring is necessary from each valve to the controller.

Drip Irrigation

Originally developed in Israel for agriculture, drip irrigation is an extremely efficient water-delivery system. A small volume of water is delivered under low pressure to each plant. The water slowly drips into the root zone allowing the plant ample opportunity to absorb the maximum amount. There is little waste.

Using rigid PVC pipe throughout the irrigation system will reduce maintenance.

FIGURE 10: ***Single-outlet Emitter Layout for Shrubs and Multi-outlet Emitter Layout for Trees.***

For most shrubs and groundcovers, one single-outlet emitter with an output of 1 gallon per hour is adequate.

Emitter should be located on uphill side of plant rootball 6" from plant center. See Figures 11 and 12 for placement of tree emitters.

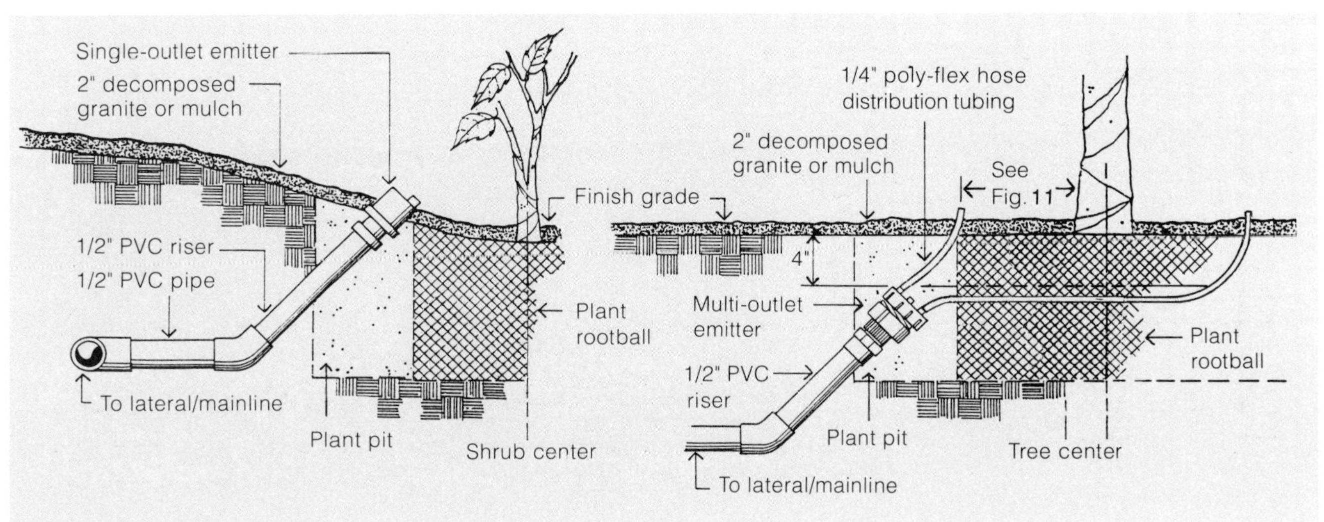

Tree Size	Number of Multi-Outlet Emitters/ Outlet Flow	Distance from Trunk 1st Outlets	2nd Outlets
<48" box	2 - 1 gph	4 @ 18"	8 @ 54"
48-60" box	2 - 2 gph	4 @ 18"	6 @ 54"
>60" box	3 - 2 gph	6 @ 30"	12 @ 66"

FIGURE 11: ***Minimum Emitter Requirements for Tree Rootball.*** *Place emitters slightly closer together for sandy soil and farther apart for soil with high-clay content. See Figure 12 for additional emitters needed for root-growth area.*

Boxes less than 48" use two multi-outlet emitters of 1 gallon per hour capacity.

Multi-outlet emitters deliver water to the plant at various locations through distribution tubing.

You'll get bigger, healthier and longer-lived trees by using the oprimum emitter layout in Figure 12.

The only way to install the entire optimum emitter layout is at initial installation. Mature shrubs and groundcover will make it almost impossible to accomplish later.

Although the equipment has been upgraded for permanent installation in the landscape, a wide variation in quality, accuracy and reliability still exists. Choosing the cheapest materials will be more costly over time due to repairs, replacement of parts and plant loss and replacement.

After the valve, all drip zones need a wye strainer to filter out debris and a pressure regulator to ensure low pressure in the line. At the end of each line a flush plug facilitates purging the line of debris during maintenance or in case of breaks. This will help to keep the tiny outlets in the emitters from clogging with debris. Self-flushing emitters reduce maintenance. The wye strainer, pressure regulator and flush plug should all be installed below grade in valve boxes. Don't crowd equipment in valve boxes as it will make maintenance difficult.

Sometimes in an attempt to reduce costs, poly-tubing is used for lateral lines on drip systems. The use of rigid PVC pipe will provide the most trouble-free and enduring system. In areas where rocks and rodents abound, only PVC piping should be considered. The mainline should always be PVC pipe.

In orchards or designs with numerous trees in close proximity, it is practical to place the trees and shrubs on separate valves. The trees can be irrigated at infrequent intervals for long duration to encourage deep root growth. Shrubs and groundcover can be watered more frequently to accommodate their shallower root systems.

Usually, trees are interspersed among shrubs and groundcovers, making it impractical to provide separate valves for each plant type. Trees, shrubs and groundcover all have different root depths and different irrigation needs. It is not possible to select plants from these categories for a combination with identical water needs.

Large boxed trees, whether salvaged or nursery-grown, have the greatest water need. Small shrubs and groundcover generally have the least. Fortunately, manufacturers have recognized the need for emitters with varied gallonage output. Select equipment carefully and you can meet the needs of all your plants.

Scheduling is an important factor when selecting equipment. Use Figure 13 only as a guideline. It is necessary to know the watering preferences of each plant. Soil type plays an important role as well.

For most shrubs and groundcover one single-outlet emitter with an output of 1 gallon per hour is adequate. Provide one emitter for each plant.

Drip Irrigation for Trees

Each tree needs a minimum of two or three multiple-outlet emitters with an output of 1 to 2 gallons per hour for each outlet. (See section on scheduling and Figures 11 and 12.)

Contrary to popular belief, roots cannot "smell" water and grow out to meet it. They require consistent moisture to develop their full potential and to extend or grow through surrounding soil.

Recent research on tree growth has shown that roots extend more than 1-1/2 times the plant's diameter. In other words, if a tree's canopy is normally 20' at maturity, feeder roots will reach a diameter of 30' or more. The majority of roots are found within 3-4' of the surface.

This information can be applied to landscape and irrigation design, not only to conserve water, but to provide optimum conditions for tree growth. Traditionally, landscape professionals have recommended

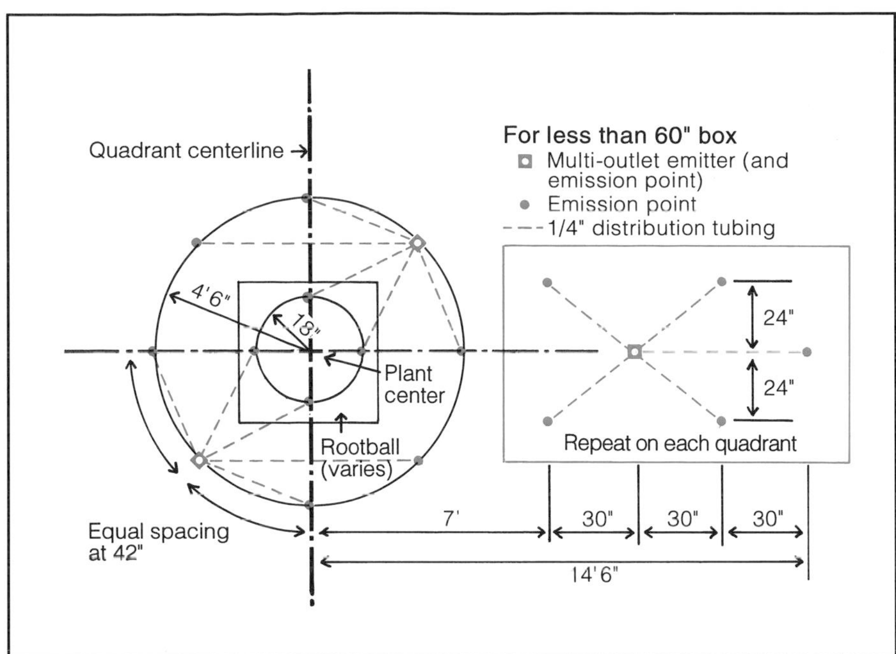

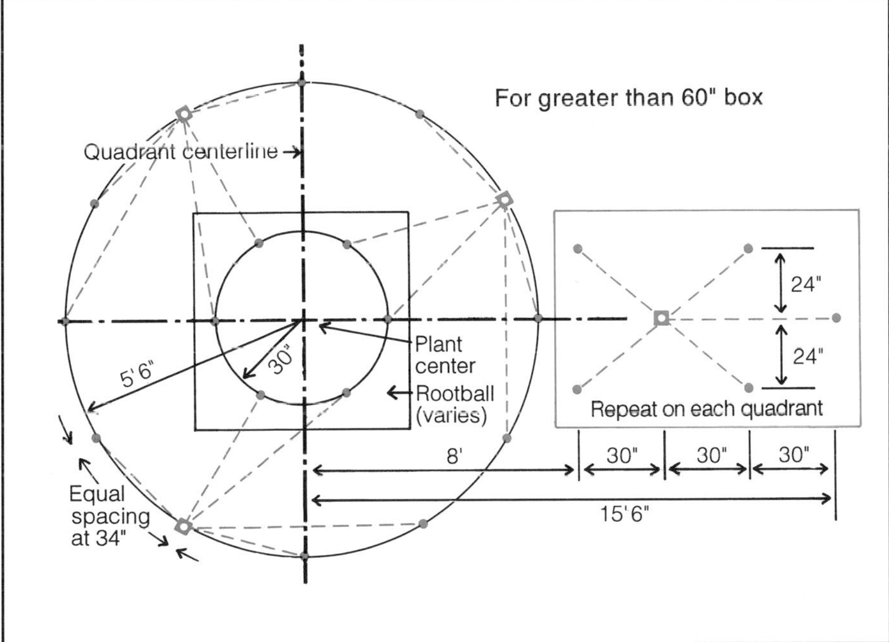

FIGURE 12: ***Optimum Emitter Layout for Trees*** *Emitter-tubing emission points should be equally spaced and located to direct flow to plant rootball. Measurement and exact placement of emission points is essential to prevent dry patches through which roots cannot grow. For any desired emission point outside the rootball area that coincides with a shrub location, use a single-outlet emitter and PVC lateral.*

(Top) For trees in less than 5-ft. boxes, locate two multi-outlet emitters 4 ft. 6 in. from plant center with four emission points at 1 ft. 6 in. from center and eight at 4 ft. 6 in. from center. Locate four more outer emitters at 90° angles from plant at a distance of 9 ft. 6 in.— or a combination of single- and multi-outlet emitters— arranged so emission points circle the tree every 2 ft. 6 in. out from tree center. This encourages broader root growth to prevent trees from blowing over.

(Left) For trees in boxes larger than 5 ft., locate three multi-outlet emitters so emission points circle the rootball twice, once at a 2-ft. 6-in.radius from tree center and again at 5 ft 6 in. Place four outer emitters at a distance of 10 ft. 6 in.from plant center—or a combination of single- and multi-outlet emitters—so emission points circle the tree every 2 ft. 6 in. out from tree center. This encourages broader root growth to prevent trees from blowing over.

(Below) The four rectangles represent the placement of the optimum emitter layout. Each rectangle is on a quadrant centerline around the rootball.

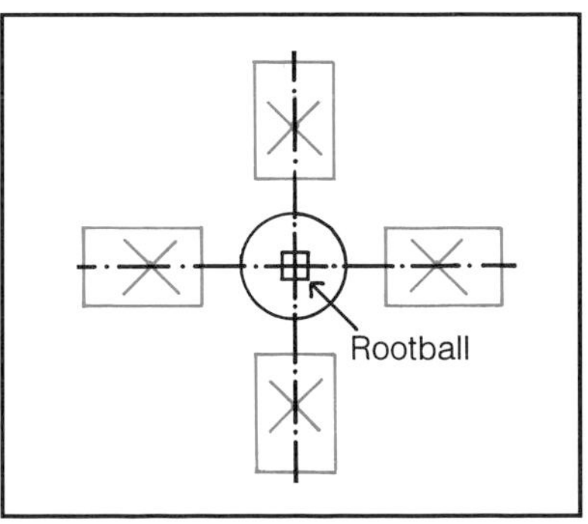

providing irrigation to the drip line (edge of the canopy), but new findings indicate the need to extend irrigation from the drip line to at least another 50% of the diameter of the mature tree (25% on each side).

Instead of progressively adding irrigation to accommodate root growth, plan ahead by installing the entire system necessary to ensure success at the time of landscaping. It is hard to add on later (why dig up lawn or groundcover) and no one ever does anyway. Provide irrigation to the rootball and *throughout the area of root growth*. (See Figure 12.)

Vary the number of emission points with drought tolerance and foliage density. Use four rays minimum. Run one ray completely across the future root zone in the direction of prevailing winds.

Trees "shoe-horned" into tiny openings in concrete have no future. It is no wonder that there is such a high mortality rate for urban trees—nationwide, less than 13 years life expectancy.

Using the emitter locations for trees (Figure 12) will produce stronger, healthier trees.

When the weather changes, change the irrigation programs.

Colorful plants in pots or containers can be moved wherever needed to provide color for accents. Simplify pot watering by using emitters that are part of your drip-irrigation system.

Drip-irrigation Pointers

Older irrigation systems incorporating bubblers and shrub sprays can be converted to drip for greater efficiency. Each plant will need an emitter. Hardware such as a wye strainer and a pressure regulator must be added.

Each plant needs its own emitter. Place emitter uphill from plant, within 6" of rootball for shrubs and groundcover and a minimum of 18" from a tree trunk. (Fig. 10, 12.)

Spaghetti on multi-port emitters should be placed under minimum 2" soil to stabilize location. Refer to section on scheduling for placement of outlets. Leave 1" of spaghetti exposed.

When using poly-tubing, bury it as you would PVC pipe to reduce maintenance and prolong life.

Bubblers

Seasonal flowers thrive best in level beds watered with bubblers. Flowers require more water than permanent plantings. In this example many emitters would be needed to provide even moisture to all plants. In sloped areas, basins are required to keep irrigation water from bubblers in the plant-root zone. Basins are not particularly attractive. On steep slopes, basin washout is a maintenance problem. For most applications, bubblers are an inefficient choice.

For improved water conservation in older landscapes, convert the bubbler system to emitters. Add risers so each plant will have its own emitter. Place emitters so entire root zone can be watered. Refer to the section on drip irrigation for a list of the additional hardware required on a drip system.

Shrub Sprays

The most practical use of shrub sprays is on plantings of seasonal flowers in sloped beds. Flowers may grow tall and block the spray. The result is dry areas which don't perform well. Flowers and foliage may be damaged by the spray. Other negatives with shrub sprays are: a high evaporation rate, unsightly appearance and their vulnerability to vandals. Using pop-up sprays will eliminate the last two problems.

Poly-tubing and Leaky Hoses

These products are most successful when use is limited to temporary installations such as seasonal flowers or vegetable gardens. They are easily damaged or clogged. The great flexibility of this piping is an advantage over PVC pipe. The ability to remove the irrigation line easily during work is an advantage in areas that are frequently dug up.

Irrigation Scheduling

A plant's life in the landscape can be divided into three stages: establishment, growth and maintenance.

Establishment

The establishment period follows installation and overlaps the first portion of the growth period. Recent university studies indicate that establishment (achieving balance in dry weight between roots and branches) takes three to five years.

Usually we recognize an initial establishment period of two to three months. Plants are most sensitive to watering during this period because all existing roots have been developed in the rootball within the nursery container. It is necessary to maintain sufficient moisture within the rootball to maintain plant health. Moisture outside the rootball is necessary to encourage root growth out into the soil.

After two to three months, the watering schedule can be reduced somewhat, but keep in mind the longer, true establishment period.

Determining an appropriate irrigation schedule during this period is tricky. Wind, air temperature, humidity and type of soil impact irrigation needs. If the soil is sandy, as in the Coachella Valley, frequent irrigation is needed. Soils with high-clay content retain moisture better. Irrigation in clay soils is needed less frequently than in sandy soils.

Established Plants	Season	Frequency in days	Duration and Penetration
Summer lawns	Summer Spr & Fall Winter	1-5 3-5 20-30	1/2 to 1 hour, maintain soil moisture at least 12" deep
Winter lawns	Spr & Fall Winter	3-5 5-10	1/4 to 3/4 hour, maintain soil moisture 8 to 10" deep
Trees in grass lawns	Summer Spr & Fall Winter	5-10 5-10 14-21	4 to 6 hours, maintain soil moisture 3 to 4' deep
Trees in Xeriscapes	Summer Spr & Fall Winter	3-10 10-14 30-60	4 to 6 hours, maintain soil moisture 3 to 4' deep
Desert trees	April-Nov	15-30	2 to 3 hours, maintain moisture 2 to 3' deep
Shrubs, vines hedges in Xeriscapes	Summer Spr & Fall Winter	3-5 5-10 14-21	1 to 2 hours, maintain soil moisture 2 to 3' deep
Cacti	May-Oct	monthly to maintain appearance	1/4 to 1/2 hour
Seasonal flowers in ground	Summer Spr & Fall Winter	2-3 3-5 5-7	1/4 to 1/2 hour, maintain soil moisture 12 to 15" deep
Vegetable Gardens	Summer Spr & Fall Winter	2-3 3-5 5-7	1/4 to 1/2 hour, maintain soil moisture 15 to 20" deep
Indoor container plants	Summer Spr & Fall Winter	5-7 3-5 5-7	until water drains out of container bottom
Outdoor container plants	Summer Spr & Fall Winter	3-5 3-5 5-7	until water drains out of container bottom

New Plantings	Season	Frequency in days	Duration and Penetration
Seeds	Year-round	don't allow soil surface to dry	maintain moist soil surface through seedling establishment
Transplants	Year-round	enough to minimize foliage wilt	thoroughly moisten root zone

FIGURE 13: ***Watering Schedules.*** *General guidelines for watering landscape plants in southern and central Arizona and southern California. Adjust your schedule to weather conditions, plant appearance and salt-leaching requirements.*

Established landscapes and plants sensitive to summer watering should be watered for the same duration but less frequently. Don't water excessively!

Palms, junipers, cypress and pines may need more frequent winter watering.

Summer lawns need lawn sprayers. Trees, shrubs, vines, hedges and vegetable gardens need emitters. Seasonal flower gardens should have bubblers.

Growth

The next stage is growth. You want the landscape to mature rapidly for aesthetics and environmental benefits but not so rapidly that root growth is sacrificed for excessive, top-heavy and tender foliage.

During this period the plants need regular, deep irrigations to maintain active growth until they reach the desired size. Don't over-water! The growth period for trees will extend beyond the establishment period.

Maintenance

Maintenance is the longest stage in a plant's life. Once it has become established and reached the desired size, irrigation can be adjusted to maintain health but not encourage growth. You will need to experiment to learn the proper scheduling for

Signs of Drought-Stress

- Morning wilt is easily noticeable.
- Dull foliage color and lack of luster
- Lack of new growth during warm season
- Foliage drop other than normal winter dormancy
- Leaf and branch tip damage
- Foliage feels warm to the touch.
- Loss of crispness
- Smaller leaf size than normal
- Shortening of internodes (the space between leaves)
- Curling leaves
- Yellowing of foliage
- Leaves of Aloe and Agave and the branches of some shrubs curve upward and inward to reduce the water loss by evapo-transpiration.
- Insects infest weakened plants.
- Footprints remain in lawn. Shaded areas may be OK.

each season. Make notes as to what works. Observe the plants often, particularly during warm weather to be sure the schedule is working. In addition to water savings you will have less pruning to do.

Early evening is the best time to water because lower temperatures and higher humidity are combined with cooling soil. This tends to pull the water down where it will be protected from evaporation the following day.

Seasonal Variations

The water requirements of plants also vary with the seasons. Summer irrigation schedules are the most difficult. During the warm season the high evapotranspiration rate can cause plants great stress.

Sufficient water must be available to the roots. However, the combination of high temperatures and excessive moisture encourages the growth of microorganisms (such as water molds) which may kill plants with root decay.

As the roots die, the foliage cannot receive the moisture it needs. Because of this, the visible effects of root decay on foliage resemble those caused by drought-stress. An overwatered plant will collapse suddenly, however, and a drought-stressed plant will gradually decline.

Detecting Drought-Stress in Plants

My friend Ron Gass once told me, "You don't have to talk to your plants. But if you're close enough to talk to them you ought to notice a lot." Observation is the key to detecting drought-stress and other potential problems. Be aware of the appearance of healthy, unstressed plants so you can identify early drought-stress.

Plants display drought-stress in different ways. Established and newly installed plants withstand varying degrees of drought differently. Minimal drought will not affect fullness of leaf or flowering in established plants. Compare the plant being observed to its context. Is it new or established? Are most of the others doing well?

Plants that have been grown in large containers take longer to establish than plants from smaller ones. Fall is the least-stressful planting season for most plants. With a proper irrigation system, year-round planting is successful.

Pleasing juxtaposition of plant colors ties in nicely with house and rock colors.

Index

Abyssinian acacia 6-7, 102
Acacia 6-11
  A. abyssinica 6, 7, 102
  A. aneura 6-7, 102
  A. berlandieri 6-7, 102
  A. farnesiana 9
  A. greggii 101
  A. rigens 7, 106
  A. salicina 8, 102
  A. smallii (minuta) 8-9, 102
  A. stenophylla 10, 102
  A. willardiana 11, 102
African aloe 15, 112, 116
Agave 12-13
  A. bovicornuta 12, 116
  A. colorata 12, 116
  A. parryi 13, 116
  A. vilmoriniana 13, 116
Ajamete 19, 116
Aloe 14-15
  A. barbadensis (A. vera) 15, 112, 116
  A. ferox 15
  A. saponaria 14, 15, 112, 116
Anacahuita 32, 33, 106
Anigozanthos flavidus 16, 116
Aniscanthus quadrifidus 16-17, 106
Antigonon leptopus 18, 120
Aquilegia chrysantha 18-19, 116
Argentine mesquite 75, 103
Arizona mesquite 76, 103
Arizona rosewood 92, 110
Asclepias subulata 19, 116
Asclepias tuberosa 19, 116
Asparagus densiflorus 'Myers' 20, 112, 116
Autumn sage 82, 109
Baccharis sarothroides 'Centennial' 20, 21, 112
Bahia absinthifolia 21
Baileya multiradiata 20-21, 112
Baja-red fairy duster 24-25, 106, 116
Baja ruellia 80, 109
Bamboo, heavenly 62, 108
Bamboo muhly 61, 117
Banana yucca 98, 119
Beard yucca 99, 119
Beardtongue 70
Beavertail prickly pear 66, 118
Bees 8, 26, 28, 76, 80
Berlandier acacia 6-7, 102
Berlandiera lyrata 22, 116
Bird of paradise 24, 106
Black dalea 34, 107
Blackfoot daisy 60, 112, 117
Blue Ranger 56, 108
Blue yucca 97, 98, 119
Bougainvillea brasiliensis 22, 106, 112, 120, 127
Brahea armata 23, 102
Brahea edulis 23, 102
Brittlebush 40, 107
Buckhorn cholla 66, 118
Bull grass 61, 118
Butterfly weed 19, 116
Caesalpinia 24, 102, 106
  C. cacalaco 24, 102
  C. gilliesii 24, 106
  C. mexicana 24, 106
  C. pulcherrima 24, 106
Caliche, planting in 129
California fan palm 96-97, 104
California fuschia 99, 113
Calliandra 24-25
  C. californica 24-25, 106, 116
  C. eriophylla 25, 106
  C. peninsularis 25
Calylophus hartwegii 'Sierra Sundrop' 25, 116
Canyon penstemon 71, 118
Cascalote 24, 102
Cassia 26-27
  C. artemisioides 26, 106
  C. biflora 26, 106
  C. candolleana 26, 106
  C. goldmanii 26, 106
  C. nemophila 27, 106
  C. phyllodenia 27, 106
  C. wislizenii 27, 106
Cat's-claw vine 58, 59, 120
Cenizo 53-55, 108
Centennial 20, 21, 112
Cercidium 28-29
  C. floridum 28-29, 102
  C. microphyllum 28, 102
  C. praecox 28-29, 102
Cereus hildemannianus 30, 116
Chaparral sage 81, 109
Chaste tree 95, 104, 110
Cherry-red sage 81, 109
Chihuahuan sage 54, 56, 108
Chilean mesquite 76, 103
Chilopsis linearis 30-31, 102
Chinese elm 91, 104
Chocolate flower 22, 116
Cholla 66-67
Chorisia speciosa 32, 102
Christmas cholla 67, 118
Chunari 46, 117
Chuparosa 50, 107
Coahuilan hesperaloe 49, 117
Colorado mesquite 75, 103
Columbine 18, 19, 116
Compact Texas sage 53, 108
Compass Barrel 45, 117
Cooba 8, 102
Coral gum 42, 103
Coral vine 18, 120
Cordia boissieri 32, 33, 106
Cordia parvifolia 32-33, 107
Cowshorn agave 12, 116
Creosote 51, 107
Cycas revoluta (cycad) 33, 116
Dahlberg daisy 36-37, 112
Dalea 34-35
  D. frutescens 'Sierra Negra' 34, 107
  D. greggii 34, 107, 112
  D. pulchra 34-35, 107
  D. versicolor 35, 107
Dasylirion acrotriche 35, 116
Dasylirion wheeleri 35, 117
Date palm 72, 103, 119
Deer grass 61, 118
Deer vetch 57, 117
Desert, definition of 2
Desert bird of paradise 24, 106
Desert broom 20, 21, 112
Desert cassia 27, 106
Desert Christmas cholla 67, 118
Desert fern 58, 103, 108
Desert ironwood 65, 103
Desert mallow 86, 110, 119
Desert marigold 20-21, 112
Desert milkweed 19
Desert spoon 35, 116, 117
Desert sweet acacia 8-9, 102
Desert willow 30-31, 102
Dietes bicolor 36, 117
Dietes vegeta 36, 117
Diez en la mañana 48-49, 117
Dodonaea viscosa 36-37, 107
Drought, overall effects of 2
Drought-stress in plants 136
Dyssodia pentachaeta 36-37, 112
Easter-lily cactus 39, 117
Echinocactus grusonii 38, 117
Echinocereus engelmannii 38-39, 117
Echinopsis multiplex 39, 117
Emitters, irrigation
  installation 134
  layout 130, 133
  requirements 132
  self-flushing 132
Encelia farinosa 40, 107
Engelmann's prickly pear 67, 118
Eremophila decipiens 40, 107
Eremophila glabra 'Murchison River' 40, 107
Ericameria laricifolia 40, 107
Esperanza 88-89, 110, 120
Eucalyptus 41-43
  E. erythrocorys 41, 102
  E. formanii 42, 102
  E. leucoxylon 'Rosea' 42, 102
  E. spathulata 42, 102
  E. torquata 42, 103
  E. woodwardii 43, 103
Euphorbia 44
  E. biglandulosa 44
  E. myrsinites 44, 112
  E. rigida 44, 112
Evapotranspiration 126
Evergreen elm 91, 104
Evergreen iris 36, 117
Fairy duster 24-25, 106, 116
Feather bush 58, 103, 108
Feathery cassia 26, 106
Fendler's penstemon 70-71, 118
Ferocactus acanthodes 45, 117
Ferocactus wislizenii 45, 117
Firecracker penstemon 70, 118
Fish-hook barrel 45, 117
Flowered gum 42-43
Forman's eucalyptus 42, 102
Fortnight Lily 36, 117
Fouquieria splendens 46-47, 107
Fouquieria macdougalii 46, 117
Foxtail fern 20, 112, 116
Gazania rigens 'Sun Gold' 48, 112
Globe mallow 86, 110, 119
Glochid removal 66
Golden barrel cactus 38, 117
Golden fleece 36-37, 112
Golden ball lead tree 52, 103
Golden-spurred columbine 18-19, 116
Goldman's cassia 26, 106
Goodding verbena 93, 113
Green Cloud sage 53-54, 108
Green waste 4
Groundcover(s) 15, 20, 34, 40, 48, 51, 60, 62, 64, 66, 80, 82, 111-113
  compared to lawn 124-125
Guadalupe palm 23, 102
Guajillo 6-7, 102
Haplopappus laricifolia 40, 107
Heavenly bamboo 62, 108
Hedgehog cactus 38-39, 117
Hesperaloe 49
  H. funifera 49, 117
  H. nocturna 49, 117
  H. parviflora 49, 117
Hildmann's cereus 30, 116
Hop bush 36, 37, 107
Horticulture 122-137
Housing production 122
Hummingbird trumpet 99, 113
Hummingbirds 5, 14-17, 19, 25, 40, 42, 49-51, 81, 87, 99
Illarie 41, 102
Indian fig 66, 103
Ipomea carnea 48, 50, 117
Irrigation 125, 127, 129-136
  bubblers 134
  components schematic 131
  controllers 131
  drip 132-134
  flush plug 132
  mainline 129-130
  maintenance 127
  old systems improvement 131
  Phoenix home-irrigation study 125
  poly-tubing for 132, 134
  scheduling 134-135
  shrub sprays 134
  system 129-134
  vacuum breaker 130-31
  valves 131-132
  wye strainer 131-132, 134
  See also Emitters, irrigation
Jojoba 84, 109
Joshua tree 98, 104
Juicy Fruit gum, fragrance of 85
Justicia californica 50, 107
Justicia spicigera 50, 105, 107, 112
Kangaroo paw 16, 116
Lady Bank's rose 79, 120
Landscape zones 123-124
Lantana 50-51, 107, 112
Larrea divaricata 51, 107
Lavender orchid vine 59, 120
Lechuiguilla verde 12, 116
Lemon-flowered gum 43, 103
Leucaena retusa 52, 103

Leucophyllum 53-56
L. candidum 53, 107
L. frutescens 53-55, 108
L. laevigatum 55-56, 108
L. langmaniae 'Rio Bravo' 55, 108
L. pruinosum 'Sierra Bouquet' 55, 108
L. 'Rain Cloud' 55-56, 108
L. zygophyllum 'Blue Ranger' 56, 108
Lindheimer muhly 61, 118
Little-leaf cordia 32-33, 107
Lophocereus schotti forma monstrosus 56-57, 117
Lotus rigidus 56-57, 117
Lyre leaf 22, 116
Lysiloma microphyllum 58, 103, 108
Macfadyena unguis-cati 58-59, 120
Mascagnia lilacina 59, 120
Mascagnia macroptera 59, 120
Mealy-cup sage 82, 109
Medicinal aloe (vera) 15, 112, 116
Melampodium leucanthum 60, 112, 117
Merremia aurea 60, 120
Mescal bean 84-85, 104, 109
Mescal ceniza 12, 116
Mesquite 75-76, 103
Mexican bird of paradise 24, 106
Mexican blue palm 23, 102
Mexican blue sage 81, 109
Mexican buckeye 92, 104
Mexican ebony 73, 103
Mexican evening primrose 64, 112
Mexican fan palm 96, 104
Mexican Flame 16-17, 106
Mexican honeysuckle 50, 107, 112
Mexican organ pipe 69, 118
Mexican sage 83, 109
Mexican tarragon 88, 119
Milkweed 19, 116
Monk's pepper tree 95, 104, 110
Morning glory 60, 120
Mt. Atlas anise 88, 119
Mountain Flame 17, 106
Mountain marigold 88, 119
Muhly 61, 117, 118
Muhlenbergia 61
M. dumosa 61, 118
M. emersleyi 61, 117
M. lindheimeri 61, 118
M. rigens 61, 118
Mulch 125, 130
Mulga 6, 7, 102
Murchison River 40, 107
Myer's asparagus fern 20, 112 116
Myoporum parvifolium 62, 112, 124
Nandina domestica 62, 108, 112
Narrow-leaf gimlet 42, 102
Native Americans 4, 11, 13, 46, 66-67, 75, 98
Needle acacia 7, 106
Nerium oleander 63, 108-109
New Zealand cassia 26, 106
Night-flowering hesperaloe 49, 117
Ocotillo 46-47, 107, 117
Octopus agave 13, 116
Oenothera 64
O. berlandieri 64, 112
O. caespitosa 64, 113
O. stubbii 64, 113
Oleander 63, 108-109
Olneya tesota 65, 103
Opuntia 66-68
O. acanthocarpa 66, 118
O. basilaris 66, 118
O. ficus-indica 66, 103
O. leptocaulis 67, 118
O. phaecantha 67, 118
O. robusta 67, 118
O. violacea santa-rita 68, 118
Orchid vine 59, 120
Organ pipe 69, 118
Pachycereus marginatus 69, 118
Palm
California fan 96-97, 104
Date 72, 103, 119
Guadalupe 23, 102
Mexican blue 23, 102
Mexican fan 96, 104
Sago 33, 116
Palmer's penstemon 71, 118
Palo blanco 11, 102
Palo brea 28-29, 102
Palo verde 28-29, 102
Paper flower 77, 119
Parry's agave 13, 116
Parry's penstemon 71, 118
Pea bush 34-35, 107
Pendulous yucca 98, 119
Penstemon 70-71
P. baccharifolius 70, 118
P. barbatus 70, 118
P. eatonii 70, 118
P. fendleri 70-71, 118
P. palmeri 71, 118
P. parryi 71, 118
P. pseudospectabilis 71, 118
P. spectabilis 71, 118
P. superbus 71, 119
P. thurberi 71, 119
P. wrightii 71, 119
Peruvian verbena 93, 113
Phoenix dactylifera 72, 103
Phoenix roebelenii 72, 103, 119
Pink-trumpet vine 74, 120
Pithecellobium 72-73, 103
P. flexicaule 72-73, 103
P. mexicanum 73, 103
P. pallens 73, 103
Plant selection 127
Planting 126-129
rootball care 128
shrub planting 128
tree planting 128
See also Tree staking
Plumbago scandens 74, 109
Podranea ricasoliana 74, 120
Poverty bush 40, 107
Prairie zinnia 99, 113
Prickly pear 66-68, 118
Primrose 64, 112
Prostrate myoporum 62, 112
Prosopis 75-76
P. alba 75, 103
P. chilensis 76, 103
P. glandulosa 76, 103
P. pubescens 76, 103
P. velutina 76, 103
Psilostrophe cooperi 77, 119
Psilostrophe tagetina 77, 119
Purple prickly pear 84, 118
Purple sage 83, 109
Queen's wreath 18, 120
Rain Cloud sage 56, 108
Rainfall 2
on impermeable areas 124
Red bird of paradise 24, 106
Red-cap gum 41, 102
Red Storm 83, 109
Red yucca 49, 117
Rhus ovata 78, 104, 109
Rio Bravo sage 55, 108
Rock penstemon 70, 118
Rock verbena 93, 113
Rosa banksiae lutea 79, 120
Rosmarinus officinalis (rosemary) 80, 109, 113, 119
Royal penstemon 71, 118
Ruellia peninsularis 80, 109
Sage 53-56, 81-83, 107-109
Sago palm 33, 116
Saltillo primrose 64, 112
Salvia 81-83
S. chamaedryoides 81, 109
S. clevelandii 81, 109
S. coccinea 81, 109
S. farinacea 82, 109
S. greggii 82, 88, 109
S. leucantha 83, 109
S. leucophylla 83, 109
S. microphylla 'Sierra Madre' 83, 109
San Miguelito 18, 120
Sandpaper verbena 93, 113
Scarlet bugler 70, 118
Screwbean mesquite 76, 103
Senna 26-27
S. pallida 26, 106
S. polyantha 26, 106
S. wizlizenii 27, 106
Shoestring acacia 10, 102
Shrubby cassia 27, 106
Sierra Bouquet sage 55, 108
Sierra Linda 82
Sierra Madre 83, 109
Silk-floss tree 32, 102
Silver Cloud sage 53, 107
Silver-leaf cassia 27, 106
Simmondsia chinensis 84, 109
Skeleton-leaf goldeneye 94, 110
Soap-tree yucca 98, 104, 119
Sonoran cassia 26, 106
Sonoran vitex 95, 110
Sophora secundiflora 84-85, 104, 109
Sotol 35, 117
Spanish bayonet 97, 119
Sphaeralcea ambigua 86, 110, 119
Stachys coccinea 87, 113
Stenocereus marginatus 69, 118
Staking, tree 129, 130
Sugar bush 78, 104, 109
Summer Snow 74, 109
Sun Gold 48, 112
Superb penstemon 71, 119
Tagetes lucida 88, 119
Tagetes palmeri (lemmoni) 88, 119
Tarragon 88
Tecoma stans 88, 110, 120
Tenaza 73, 103
Texas A&M Univ. 53
Texas betony 87, 113
Texas ebony 72-73, 103
Texas honey mesquite 76, 103
Texas mountain laurel 84-85, 103, 109
Texas sage 53-54, 108
Thunder Cloud sage 53, 107
Thurber's penstemon 71, 119
Tombstone Rose, The 79
Totem pole cactus 56-57, 117
Trailing indigo 34, 107, 112
Trailing lantana 50-51, 112
Tree aloe 15
Tree staking 129-130
Trichocereus candicans 90, 119
Trichocereus huascha 90-91, 119
Trumpet bush, yellow 88-89, 110, 120
Trumpet vine, pink 74, 120
Turpentine bush 40, 107
Twin-flower cassia 26, 106
Ulmus parvifolia 91, 104
Ungnadia speciosa 92, 104
Vauquelinia californica 92, 110
Velvet mesquite 76, 103
Verbena 93
V. gooddingii 93, 113
V. peruviana 93, 113
V. rigida 93, 113
V. tenera 93, 113
Viguiera stenoloba 94, 110
Vitex agnus-castus 95, 104, 110
Vitex triangularis 95, 110
Washingtonia filifera 96, 104
Washingtonia robusta 96, 104
Water use, urban 2, 4
lawn consumption 124-125
Watering schedule 134-135
Weeping wattle 8, 102
White Cloud sage 54, 108
White evening primrose 64, 113
White ironbark 42, 102
Woodward's black butt 43, 103
Wright's penstemon 71, 119
Xeriscape 2, 122-137
Yellow bells 89, 110, 120
Yellow Lady Bank's rose 79, 120
Yellow morning glory 60, 120
Yuca 60, 120
Yucca 97-99
Y. aloifolia 97, 119
Y. baccata 98, 119
Y. brevifolia 98, 104
Y. elata 98, 104, 119
Y. recurvifolia 98, 119
Y. rigida 97-98, 119
Y. rostrata 99, 119
Zauschneria californica 99, 113
Zinnia grandiflora 99